MW00977307

ANOTHER DYSFUNCTIONAL

CANCER POEM ANTHOLOGY

ANOTHER DYSFUNCTIONAL
CANCER POEM ANTHOLOGY

EDITED BY
PRISCILA UPPAL AND MEAGHAN STRIMAS

Mansfield Press

Copyright © Priscila Uppal & Meaghan Strimas 2018
All Rights Reserved
Printed in Canada

Library and Archives Canada Cataloguing in Publication

   Another dysfunctional cancer poem anthology / edited by
Priscila Uppal and Meaghan Strimas.

ISBN 978-1-77126-196-8 (softcover)

   1. Cancer--Poetry. 2. Canadian poetry (English)--21st century.
I. Uppal, Priscila, editor II. Strimas, Meaghan, 1977- editor

PS8287.C33A56 2018   C811'.60803561   C2018-905165-5

Cover Image: Shutterstock
Design and Typesetting: Denis De Klerck
Editors' Photo: Daniel Ehrenworth

The publication of *Another Dysfunctional Cancer Poem Anthology* has been generously supported by
the Canada Council for the Arts and the Ontario Arts Council.

Mansfield Press Inc.
25 Mansfield Avenue, Toronto, Ontario, Canada M6J 2A9
Publisher: Denis De Klerck
www.mansfieldpress.net

In memory of Priscila Uppal,
30 October 1974–05 September 2018

CONTENTS

WHAT DO YOU SUGGEST WE WRITE?

I just finished writing a short story called "Fuck Cancer Inc." In it, a benevolent pot-smoking failure-to-launch thirtysomething named Felix starts a T-shirt business after a conversation with his beloved aunt Lindy, who has been undergoing treatments for colon cancer:

> "If someone's going to stare at your chest, don't you want to make it worth their while, at least tell them what you're thinking, how you feel, what you wish you could say but don't have the nerve to do so. Who the fuck is Superman to you? Why do you care what happens to him? Life is too short to waste looking like a giant child. Besides, I've never seen a T-shirt that says anything I want to say."
>
> "Like what?"
>
> "Like...Fuck Cancer. I'd wear a T-shirt that said Fuck Cancer on it. But you can't buy those at the Princess Margaret Hospital gift shop, only pillowcases that say Dream Big or Princess at Rest or Hugs for Free. Now these pillowcases are ironic, Felix. They contradict everything going on in that place."

The T-shirt is a form of self-expression, I'd even venture to say poetic expression, in that it effectively and powerfully expresses experience and emotion in a non-conventional manner but on a conventional surface (here, fabric as opposed to paper).

Aunt Lindy has a bone to pick with the Spiritual Care Centre who prop up a whiteboard on an easel every morning decorated with a chosen handwritten inspirational quote that hordes of cancer patients are forced to read since it is prominently displayed in the main foyer of the biggest cancer care centre in the city. This whiteboard includes such dubious and misguided quotations as:

> *All adventures, especially into new territory, are scary.* —Sally Ride
> *Everyone smiles in the same language.* —Anonymous.
> *We are stronger as a society when old men plant trees they will never see grow.* —Wise Proverb

Fiction allows for poetic licence not afforded in the realm of journalism or non-fiction memoir, but as truth is frequently stranger than—or, at the very least, strange as—even the most comic or tragic fiction, I've had a long-standing feud with the Spiritual Care Centre at Princess Margaret Hospital in Toronto, where such a whiteboard exists and where I, and anyone accompanying me, have felt our blood boil with anger and then disbelief that anyone—let alone those apparently trained to console those who are suffering—would ever for a fleeting moment believe this whiteboard is a good idea. The quotations above are lifted verbatim from that actual whiteboard. I've explained to those in charge of the whiteboard that Sally Ride is an astronaut and she's talking about going into outer space, not undergoing invasive cancer treatments. I've also told them that they have no right to ask anyone who doesn't feel like it to smile. I won't even discuss the idiocy of posting that wise proverb before hundreds of people awaiting painful tests and treatments. It's the stuff usually touted on boards outside hairdressing salons or novelty gift stores.

In my feud, I've often turned the whiteboard around. Each time I have been rewarded with a thumbs-up from several patients (of various ages and demographics, and from the rather spritely to the haggard), approving my rebellious nature that frequently refuses to let sleeping dogs lie, as my father would say.

First, let me say that I am enormously grateful for all the work done at Princess Margaret Hospital and all cancer centres. Everyone means well. I do believe this. But that doesn't mean we shouldn't encourage improvement, progress, evolution of thought and practice. And there's not a medical professional I know who doesn't think cancer care is still fairly primitive when non-invasive efficient cures are the optimal goal (if not the abolishment of the disease in its entirety to the history books).

One of the things I've stressed in my in-person heated discussions, phone conversations, and follow-up emails with the Spiritual Care Centre staff (that have, unfortunately, as yet, gone nowhere*) is that it is *not* the job of the Spiritual Care Centre to tell (or even to suggest to) cancer patients—or their caregivers or loved ones—how they should feel or think about their experience, especially through quotations pilfered from astronauts or the prizes inside popcorn boxes.

"What do you suggest we write on the board instead?" I've been asked.

"Nothing," I've replied. (Apparently this is the worst thing you can say to people who already suspect they are doing nothing productive to help the situation. The board is a deflector, a Hail Mary pass before admitting complete defeat.)

After that initial shock, I elaborate. "You should let the patients speak for themselves. Give them markers to write how they feel on the whiteboard."

But of course—and I've said so—they are too afraid to actually hear what we have to say. The unknown is indeed scary.

"And I think you'd be very surprised," I add.

I know I would be. And that's why I want to hear it. And why I also want to hear from caregivers and ex-lovers and surgeons and nurses and reiki practitioners and from the cafeteria and janitorial staff.

It's why I conceived of this anthology. In most situations, I enjoy being surprised. I enjoy learning and new experiences and profound visceral transformations. Cancer brings all this, too, but in a dysfunctional and terrifying way. One of our great coping mechanisms as a species is the ability to create, to express, understand, even alter our circumstances or the current structures of the world. Poetry is such a vehicle. As is humour. As is friendship. As is empathy. As is witnessing. As is invention. As is hope.

I was compelled to write "Fuck Cancer Inc." just as I was compelled to write "Another Dysfunctional Cancer Poem," the poem that inspired the title for the anthology. I didn't set out to write a "cancer story" or "cancer poem"—in fact, I think the titles infer the opposite, or at least an uneasy relationship with the subject. (In art, as in life.) We write what we are compelled to write, not what others suggest we should write.

When Felix creates his first Fuck Cancer T-shirt, it's a gift of expression to his beloved aunt Lindy and then to a much wider community. But it doesn't stop there. Even Aunt Lindy can't have the last word (or the last T-shirt, in this case). Felix finds himself making more and more T-shirts, with more and more things people wish they could say and write. And while Meaghan and I have collected over a hundred poems in *Another Dysfunctional Cancer Poem Anthology*, we received hundreds more. And there are hundreds, thousands, perhaps millions more out there. All deserve their own whiteboards.

Priscila Uppal

Coda: *I am pleased to report that since I wrote this introduction, the Spiritual Care Centre staff have recently removed the offensive whiteboard, and we are in correspondence about ways to empower cancer patients, caregivers, and staff through literary expression, rather than creating more alienation. I am hopeful that this anthology—and future books devoted to exploring an array of responses and experiences to this ubiquitous disease—will be part of a compassionate movement whereby literature and health care work beneficially together to advocate for all that is compassionate and human.

About two years ago my husband was diagnosed with throat cancer. When his call came, I was sitting in a noisy café with a friend. On the phone, he was all business—no "Hello" or "How are you?" He asked me to move somewhere quiet: he had something important to tell me. I remember stepping outside, my hand on the glass door. The sharp winter air making my eyes water. He told me that the lump on his neck we'd both dismissed—but agreed he should get checked—contained cancerous cells. At the time, he had no real idea how bad it was. I remember falling to my knees. I was on the ground, but I felt as if I were floating. The cancer had entered his body, and I left mine. We were both unmoored.

Cancer is the worst kind of house guest: it arrives unannounced and unwelcome—and it overstays. It robs you, fills each room with drama and anguish, and then wrecks the furniture. You hate it so much that you can't bear to make eye contact. Sometimes the disease is sneaky: it turns back the clocks or moves them ahead. It's not enough that cancer invades your body; no, it has to toy with your head as well.

My husband stayed blessedly level and strong during this awful time, but there was a downside to his tenacity. In the early days of his treatment, he believed he would "sail through" unscathed. And he managed for a while, but after a few weeks, he began literally starving to death. He couldn't swallow and his throat and mouth filled up with a sticky, thick mucous that made him feel like he was constantly drowning on dry ground. He was skeletal and on the verge of kidney failure. I am ashamed to admit that, for some time, I was also in denial. Neither of us was thinking clearly, but thankfully my younger sister, who works in health care, demanded I advocate for him, and he was soon fitted with a feeding tube, something I think we had resisted because it made our new existence so terribly real.

I was not myself during this time. I was looking after our baby boy, in my first year of a new career as a full-time college professor. I was wracked with fear and guilt. And I was irrationally angry—angry with my husband because I felt abandoned. His getting sick was not part of our deal. I needed him. I needed his help. There was a morning when I was running late for work. I had just dropped our son off at daycare and I had to be in the classroom within the hour. Traffic was bad. As I waited in a line of cars, I watched as a police officer escorted a group of children, colourful little beings in bright hats and scarves and mitts, across the road. And for reasons I only now understand, I impatiently honked my horn. The police officer approached and knocked on my window. Panicked, I explained that I was late for work. I told her I hadn't slept in days. She was not impressed. And I was horrified by my behaviour. It was so unlike me. Now I see this moment for what it was: I was begging to be stopped. I wanted her attention. For the rest of the drive, I screamed. It was an uncontrollable noise that came from deep within my body. It was me—and it was not me.

Miraculously, my husband recovered—though not without nearly dying of a chemo-related pulmonary embolism and having parts of his body permanently damaged by the treatment. Our lives are, mostly, back to normal. But they will never be the same. Cancer may leave the body, but once it visits a house, it always lingers on the doorstep.

And that girlfriend who was with me in the café the day my husband told me his news? Earlier this year she called me to say she'd just been given the results of a biopsy. Cancer had found her, too.

Cancer is ubiquitous. And this is why we need to find comfort when and where we can. We who have had it, or have lived through the hell of watching loved ones struggle with it, need to understand that we are not alone, even when we feel like we are. Priscila and I hope this anthology proves to be a friend to those who need one. Every poem in this book provides its own unique account of what it means to be "looked in on" by cancer. The selection process was a challenge: one, because there were so many worthy poems to choose from; and two, because, in reading the submissions, we had to relive moments and experiences that reflect the ruthlessness of the cancer experience. There are poems here written by mothers and daughters, poems written by fathers and sons, poems written by health-care practitioners, poems written by survivors, and, just as important, there are a few poems written by some who are now departed. And while the subject of cancer is anything but a happy one, there are many bright spots in these pages. There is even humour, an essential survival tactic when faced with a disease that aims to kill all laughter. And this is what we must hold on to—our capacity for joy, our ability to be resilient, and our readiness to reach out and establish meaningful connections that make life worth living.

Coda: Priscila conceived of this anthology in 2016, her third year of cancer treatment, as a way to create something positive out of a bad situation—an instinct that was at the core of her creative drive throughout her life. When her treatment became too onerous, she asked me to assist with putting it together. Priscila died, in Toronto's Princess Margaret Hospital, a few weeks before the book went to the printers, but was involved in its production up until the last few days of her life. I know that she desperately wanted to be here to see it out in the world, doing good and defying the odds that, ultimately, she was not able to.

Meaghan Strimas, 28 September 2018

CANCER

I'm a Cancer, born in July,
never gave it a thought. Having
cancer, something else entirely.
I imagine this crab, all claws
and sly eyes, crawling inside
me, grinning mercilessly, making
her nest of bone and bits
of undigested flesh, dreaming
her own parasitic dreams.
Should I name her, this new pet
of mine, set out bowls of warm milk,
nurture a relationship? Do crabs
like to be petted? What *do* they like?

I think of the crabs I've eaten,
soft shell, cold legs in salad,
whole Chesapeake Bay crabs,
all you can eat, served dockside
in Maryland with nutcrackers,
mallets and paper bibs, coleslaw
and fries, plenty of cold beer.
How could a pleasure so pure
come back to haunt me except
as indigestion? Surely the crabs
I've eaten have shared my joy, given
themselves up gladly. I do not,
will not. This crab must dine alone,
shuttered in darkness, far from
the sea and company of its kind.
I shed no tears for its plight,
no more than it does for mine.

IN HOSPITAL

A hospital bed is the cruellest venue.
You lie there unable to sing or dance,
your thinking cloudy. All night long,
lights never really off, you flicker through
sleep like the phantom you might well
have become, one slip of the surgeon's knife,
while a chorus line pantomimes its way
through morphine dreams. Mornings,
daylight lays a fresh coat of grey paint
across ceiling and walls as the incessant hum
rises, the poke in the arm and the catheter's
relentless tugs the only reminders you're still alive
until the breakfast wagon rolls in. Another day
to contemplate mortality or the eternity
of whatever subject comes to mind. Then,
just like Jones, along come the surgeons, a trail
of them behind one shining star, nodding his head
like the Pope, inspecting his handiwork, the postulants
nodding their heads in agreement. This is the moment
around which the day revolves, freedom or another day
pinned to the bed hang in the balance, the jangle
of the IV machine just background music.
This moment, into which the leading man steps,
your life completely in his hands, next to the scalpel.

FACING THE DIAGNOSIS, CALMLY

A bird hit the window, then flew away.
She looked up from the pages of the book.
The line of the horizon beckoned.
The worn path led to the water's edge.
Tide-smooth logs rested on the beach.
Sand piled on the shore.
Thoughts bubbled into foamy streams.
In the sky, a cloud-shaped heart.
Her breath rose and fell, deeply.
A signal fired from neuron to neuron.
Birds flitted from branch to telephone line.
Looking down, she eyed the crack in the sidewalk.
A distant dog barked as she lifted her hand.
The key fit the lock, and turned.

IRONY

"Irony is an abnormal growth."—Kierkegaard

Take a number to wait
      for the intake clerk to check
Health card, birthdate, phone numbers.
Then take another number to wait
      elsewhere to see someone
Who will see you
At some indefinite future time.
Then take a number, to wait
      to book the next appointment
To wait again.
Unless they call to change
That date to one that doesn't
Fit the calendar that counts
The number of my days.
I want to live my life
As if...
      I were more than the number
In my hand, or on the file
that defines me "patient."
      In my rich fantasy life,
I am a person
and time, it's all I have.
So...
When I take a number
      to wait,
Tell me if delays might mean
I could get a coffee
Or take a walk beside the lake.
Life seems longer,
But not better, in a waiting room.
      And will they
Call my number before
I solve the cryptic crossword clue,
"Sensitive Number"—Anaesthetic.

The poster in one waiting room says
I am an equal member of the Treatment Team,
So I must
      arrive early in time to wait.
Remember to bring the list of meds
Already detailed in your
Confidential file.
Mine not to reason why,
Mine just to do or...
      Take another number.

*

CHEWING WATER

—to Dr. Jim Wright, Juravinski Cancer Centre, Hamilton, my sister Liz Ball, and her friend Dr. Dianne Miller. I thank them for preserving my voice.

Following radiation treatment
on a cancerous vocal cord

my throat narrowed
seemed tight

I chewed water
before I could swallow it

BARBARA DYING

—my soulmate, Barbara Caruso, 1937–2009

While Barbara was in palliative care
experiencing aphasia and dementia

due to abdominal cancer
spread to her brain

I wanted her
to remain alive—

her being
in the world

was a comfort
I knew

would
vanish

SNOW

for my sister

> *"This is a winter garden. White on White.*
> *Bunches of snow like cherry on the bough."*
> —Philip Stratford, *"And Once More Saw the Stars"*

It must be a miracle.
The doctor told us
you wouldn't make the snow season.
But this year, in our warm south
winter comes earlier.
We rush to get fur coats from closets.
We are both happy and worried—
no one can predict the weather
and the future anymore.
In the news, somewhere where
there are never floods;
now it is under deep water.
When we were young,
we waited for snow eagerly.
Following you, I made snow
angels, mine always smaller.
Does it snow in heaven?
Nobody tells us.
Those who go before us, you say
go to check
and save a place for us.

CONSCRIPTED

How to make cancer a poem? The surprise of it. A sudden illness, a skeptical doctor orders tests. A week later says to get ready to spend OHIP dollars. Pancreatic cancer. Are you okay to drive home?

In the first page of my dream book, autumn is rich and putrid. Is it shameful to want to prolong a life already long, not terribly productive, full of care and caring? It seems wrong to leave new generations untethered. The nature of things. Hard, the nature of things.

The short drive home in two minds. One shocked and disbelieving. Stunned. The other watches the road, thinks, what needs to be done now? when and how should I tell them? and why not me, same as anyone?

The culture of tests—endoscopies (swallowing miniature camera and instruments), CT scans, MRIs, ultrasound. Conferences with surgical team. Before busy fugitive cells have colonized too much territory, there will be radical cutting in a Whipple operation.

Body forever different, mind slower, sluggish, after long hours of anaesthesia. Tests, fears, and alarms come and go. Is this image of the lungs evidence of metastasis? what is that shadow on the liver? Count by months, says one specialist. Let's test, says another.

One and a half years in, another three-month furlough granted between scans, permission to be temporarily absent from illness, authorized by ranks lower than the highest authority, but it's in the culture of conscripts to obey, to be glad.

Three months to occupy the strange country of the present day. Around the shops, on sidewalks, people in civvies, quick, slow, smart; rough, bright, dull. Some of the smartest-dressed fast walkers, the freshest faces, could be on furlough, too, incognito, never quite at ease.

THANKSGIVING

Their wealth of luck tugging
on their shirt sleeves, they fled
the hospital corridor.

The wild October sky. Already
they were planning, despite the storm,
to paddle through the Needle's Eye:

the channel flooded into the willow banks,
the boulders submerged. The canoe's hull
captured the heavy rain

while the wind breathed down
their backs. They wanted
to feel their lungs pushing

against their ribs
as the water splashed over
the bow.

The canoe swayed
as they stroked their way back
to their bed.

That night they woke
when the rain stopped.
They could suddenly,

after years of worry,
hear themselves think.
The world beyond the edge of their breathing:

the wind slipping
soft pine needles through
the cracks in the walls.

POST-OP DELIRIUM

Speech gasp
strangled,
surgeons' gloved hands,
screening clipboards,
clinical notes,
assault noises
and opiate waves
swim in cold and hot
flames.

I am a cocoon shroud,
lancet veins, hypodermics,
inside the steel hull
of a scanning machine,
a numbed grave,
sutured in nightshade.

My daughters running
in a topiary maze,
broken-legged dolls,
waking to dream of death
tears on my pillow,
the faint sheen of your voice.

You lean in,
your hands
unclasping mine,
I miss your body in our bed,
reach for your bent chatter,
hospital morning racket,
the walls green as absinthe,
ice chips,
press your lips to my pulse.

Dirge of idylls,
lunatic guards
in watchtowers
shock and unhinge.

My mind lost
in morphine,
in white-coated
bodies
an oxycodone scamming ring,
plotting our murder.

I try to tear out my IV tubes,
to escape,
to tell my veteran husband
the white coats want to kill us.

Code-white security:
Nurse Ann restrains
my arms cuffed to the bed.

I have rented a tomb
big enough to say final things.
Three days before I recognize anyone,
before the last unconscious hallucination
of grieving becomes
a home,
I hear lost veins singing,
burning like a novena
in my throat, heavy with thirst,
proof of life,
sure as shine

ROCK ME

Come, my daughters, come to my bedside of white sheets,
to the bindings of crib to coffin, baby bracelet to toe tag.

Rock me through this picked-to-the-bone-dry world.
Feel the objects of our lives animated by our desires.

Rock me through cities of satellites and constellations,
through the high beams of lighthouses, and trains.

Rock me through bars and coffee shops, atriums, and parks,
and through lavender and rose gardens and rot and decay.

Rock me in the comfort of clean linens.
Just as I have crawled inside of you.

Sing. Sing to your mother. Sing my name...Rishma, Rishma...
And make me a moonbeam girl—a star-child.

Rock me, so I feel myself beloved on this earth, despite
the live burial of my dreams. While broken trees

drip their leaves into my five-alarm fire—take
a filament of my hair to light your ways.

Rock me—and see how I shine through your organs
like a radiation beam.

STEREOTACTIC BIOPSY

An ink-lined box demarks the site
where the needle makes its slow descent
through my left upper lobe of breast
while a stasis of plastic plates bears down
in a prolonged mammogram.
I curb the urge to yank it out.

I can feel the lidocaine burn,
then dull pressure mounts
as the hollow needle punctures the target,
and the radiologist's fine guidance finds the cells of concern.
She says, *Don't lose too much sleep. I'm not too worried.*
Too much a recognition that sleep will be lost
among the strongest of us.
I'm not too worried supposed to soothe—
as much empathy as the doctor can dispense.

The bruise, a mutant tattoo,
tries on shades of purple and yellow,
does not mind blue ink lines
beyond which it cascades,
as if in imitation of cell division.

And the weird, deep ache—
my breast's swan song
as it abandons the possibility of lactating,
an encore—their "Swing Low, Sweet Chariot" not enough
as I circle menopause.

Now I sit and watch
the daily metastases of my bruise,
ponder the etymology of *onkos*—
the Greek word for mass, burden,
lose only a little sleep,
wait for news.

THE THORACIC SURGEON

the man is cool,
blue cool...
blue smock,
blue pants,
blue booties over shoes,
blue eyes
    —blue hair would be too much,
    invoking laughter,
    not the place for that—
he's been this way before,
many times before,
his voice so blue & cool & practised

like a squirrel
anticipating winter,
he knows the land he works,
the labour that's preceded him,
he's seen the X-rays/CTs/MRI
    —understands slow
    death by acronyming—

kneads his brow while talking
as though his words cause pain,
like needles piercing skin
    —they do, but not
    the pain he feels

dutiful & silent, patiently
we listen...
the images he flashes
in the blinding yellow light
seem sinister to untrained eyes,
but only silhouettes,
they yield imperfect insights,
best not to leap, he intimates,
into unfounded truth
as though it were a pool
    —blue as blue can be—
best to know...to know

so he will look,
with clear blue eyes,
at what is growing in your chest,
his slim blue fingers
tracing figure eights
    an inch or two above
    imagined slicing spots
    —cut here...
    & here...and here—
you jerk away,
as if his fingers might be knives,
leave them waltzing in the air

next week, perhaps the next,
he'll go to work
    —get on this, get in gear,
    clichés tumble from his lips—
mine what could be nothing,
just shadows on a screen,
but you know better,
have felt the devil lurking,
creeping through your flesh,
infecting as he goes,
tapping cryptic messages,
in the devil's own workshop

he stands, a tall man
    —even bluer at full height—
extends a hand, his handshake
like a signet ring or password
for opening a cave,
takes yours, hesitantly offered,
thanks you for your time,
for placing trust in him,
he'll do his best, he vows,
to undo fact from fiction,
bad from good,
evil from divine

THE RESPIROLOGIST

on a corner conjuring an apocalypse,
where garbage blows in drifts,
white paper sailing on the wind,
black-clad Yeshiva boys seem ghosts,
breathless loiterers
lost in reveries of *olam ha-ba*,
their empty stares, like gamma knives,
lasering the folds of space;
transported here from centuries ago,
they rock to unheard music,
back & forth, back & forth,
oblivious to the traffic, pylons to avoid

we muscle through this human wall
to the south side of the street,
where strollers wander aimlessly,
unimpressed by poorly polished shoes
worn thin from scuffing on stones,
to a windowless grey door,
climb three steep flights of stairs,
huffing, red-faced apparitions
labouring above us & below,
chests heaving with each raising of a foot,
more of life once known,
sacrificed to compromise

the walls, dull grey & pockmarked,
closed-mouthed witnesses
to battles won & lost,
judge us, then embrace us,
push us to a square, grey waiting room
where half a dozen sit, avoiding other eyes,
growing intimate with the floor
& a glassy calm that caresses like a mist;
we claim two slate-grey chairs,
the faded cushions worn out years ago,
no padding left to soften
the blows we know await us

half an hour passes,
the electric hum of flickering lights
mosquitoes through our brains,
one by one the sleepers
rise & disappear,
then, your name, a bullet fired
by a matron dipped in white;
she escorts us through the stillness
to a coffin of a room: three chairs,
a desk, a threadbare rug,
two carved grey doors,
thoracic posters on one wall

before the man appears,
another hour is lost
studying the flies hiding out in corners,
where sweat-soaked walls collide
with rust-tinged ceiling tiles;
also in white,
five foot six & balding,
he is a spectre cradling a folder,
tiny hands fondling the edge,
grey, unblinking eyes that swim,
a pencil moustache painted on,
below a hawkish nose...no chin

documents are spread before us,
x-rays held to blinding light,
a tumour on the right is clear,
its fingers stretching
like a baby's after birth;
he refers you to a surgeon,
a biopsy recommended,
& drained of words, this miniature
Tiresias offers you his hand,
unlike the tumour's almost fingerless,
motions to a greying door,
& leaves by yet another

FROM A FOOTBALL INJURY SPURRED BONE CANCER

Burrs by the hundreds, I imagined,
down his spine,
                              and here he lay,
14, in the end zone,
beneath the archway leading from the living room,

his legs pedalling
his pain,

so far downfield he was no more our cousin.

The other team had laid claim to him. His gaze
          inward; it was his model cars in his room
                              that stared
at us,
asking why he didn't sleep there,
                              and me at a loss
to explain even to
myself
                    why he preferred to be in a doorway
so that everyone must step over
him, as if he were a vacuum cleaner,
                                        his limbs every
                    which way,
mere attachments.

We'd keep to the downstairs,
where the elders
                    whispered
it was for the best—
what hung over our heads was

                    floating.

In his house,
as we poured ourselves into play,
              we found there was   always
something in the other room we wanted,

and we must step over
him yet again, as if
to our shame, it would make him smaller—
                              reduce our loss.

His hard sprint
but twitches
in his blanket now,
his body, fetal, as if he had pulled
                    that ball from the sky, buried it
in his gut.

At night sometimes his father would carry him
                                        to the window,
where he'd look for the stars.
4th down inside him,
he'd felt, maybe, the whole Colts' offence
had hit him at once—
in a high arch
he was flying back in a tackle,

                    losing

                              losing

                                   ground.

But then a strange thing: a time out,
and for days he was better—
as if Big Daddy Lipscomb did
                    what he'd often do,
reach down with a
                         gargantuan hand,
help up his opponent.

On my last visit my cousin stood up, crouched
over me in a huddle
when I had trouble with the end of his world.

He weaved
                with his
          blanket, and walked me outside,

where I looked deep into his eye
sockets, those hollows, in this overtime,
where winning isn't what you're there for.
                    He wasn't thinking of
himself
but me.

The glory of the Lord
   in his eyes,

                    he'd set down everything:
the football, his model cars, even the stars
spiralled a little tighter in the sky,

and in his eyes, deeply set, as if they were travelling back
the other way out of his head:

we sat down by a tree,
                    and though I don't know what he said,

in the flash of seconds
he spoke to me for hours.

PROCEDURE

I am down on my knees,
weeder pushed
into the throat of earth,
upending the tentacle roots
of plantain and quack grass
run rampant through the iris bed,
the basal swords of their leaves,
ragged and rusted, rhizomes
collapsed in on themselves
when the cellphone rings and rings.
The doctor's voice is
calm, precision steel.
She confirms the diagnosis,
hard facts I only
partially absorb,
though cancer and larynx
have the grind of a knife.
She describes the protocol
for treatment.
I turn off the phone, lean back on my heels,
breathe deeply, observe the dry stone wall
circling the iris bed built with field rock
from the abandoned foundation
of my grandmother's family home,
the granite boulders I dug out
below this earth, using an iron bar
to pry them from where
they had lain for centuries.

I bend forward, continue to pick over,
a procedure that must be done
if the irises are to remain vigorous.
Early stage, she had said,
good prognosis. Her insistence,
her reassurance, the warmth
of this soil on my hands.
Next year's promise of flowering
by severing out the rot.

RETURN TO ST. JOSEPH'S

Approaching Parkside from
the park, I spot the cross
above where, seven months
ago, they took me in.
Twelve hours of shooting
skeletal pain with nothing
but a saline drip and a single
cup of water that tasted
thick. They mapped my insides
out with dyes and rays. Before
I was conveyed into a half-
million-dollar cross between
a pop can and coffin,
the lab tech kindly placed
a lead shield over my crotch.
Earlier, walking past triage,
she'd given me this look
like, *You howling, screw-
faced junkie, you won't
get to me.* So why the change
in disposition? Was
the morphine kicking in?
I had questions about organ
donation and who I was
supposed to call first.

TRANSFUSION

I walk most days before dinner now
that the air is finally calm and clear,
and each time the horizon admits more
of the visible world. The windowsills are lined

with potted herbs. Fleets of rental toilets
are converging on the park, where blue squills
bloom like dye in water. Welcome
to the party: an ache in my head I could
crawl up into, abetted by spring rot.

Curious provisional sprouts betray
the dreaded taproot, but I'll clear the yard
for pole beans and baby beets, keen
as the Sun-Maid girl, O Spring, if you
promise me more light and good clean blood.

RADIANT

In his white coat the radiologist jokes:
we're in the bat cave in here.

The dark room, its thick metal door,
and when inside a sense of backstage, of secrecy—

the table in the centre; a slab
where you might expect Frankenstein,

hair on end, pink and green smoke
spiralling from his test tubes.

You climb on, compliant, and they begin
their measuring, their math-chat,

red lights tack your torso as if for a plane's landing.
You are a runway. Bisected and branded, you

keep still. Stretch your arms behind
to hold the pole, brace like a stripper—

your exposed breasts scarred like hers, too.
The machine's swivelling eye

directs itself and when they turn it on
the red buzzer blares its loud applause

for how well you receive this toxic cure,
how well you hold the pose.

THE SUMMER I'M TEN MY AUNT WEARS A BRIGHT BLUE SHIRT

She wears it everywhere this year,
even swimming,
to cover where there used to be a breast.

What must it look like, a chest with only one?
I try to imagine, peek down her front
or up her sleeve,

sneak into the bedroom when she's changing
but she's fast,
and all I see is her bright blue shirt.

SHEET MUSIC FOR BREATHING IN THE RADIATION ROOM
after John Cage

Ratchet silence, I hear ammunition hammer.
Go on, health is a backwards trip. Yelps

before baby steps, tantrums, kicking candy
in the hourglass. Hex and melt each fixin'.

Toss the mulch of yes. Hush and play *4'33"*
under the spell she was. Don't melt. Don't.

Question the tunnel. Horse-throw black cattle.
Terraform black suns of stemmed plucked flowers.

Let mother's hands play trickster the bird before
a plenary nap. Let scorched petals fall at your feet.

MRI

No metal implants or fragments.
A long, fibrous stalk.
You signed consent, removed jewellery.
Face down through the doughnut hole.
Tapering into leaves.
Contrast material running through your veins.
Magnets. Pinnate to bipinnate with rhombic leaflets.
Still—lie still.
You've been given earphones, a padded table.
Seeds are broad ovoids.
Cushioned openings for breasts to hang.
Grown in an open garden.
Thumping. Clicking. Knocks and taps.
The celery's a cleansing tonic.
Whirs with car-accident screeches—
a father's skull, mother's mouth.
Wide range of cultivars.
The technician stands in a nearby room.
Inside, a seed; inside, a small fruit.

THE MALIGNANT MANDARIN: HAIBUN

"The PET scan lights up all the cancer colonies," the surgeon tells her. And then he points to the computer screen. "Your tumour is the size of a mandarin orange." He drones away in a clinical voice about radiation and cure rates, as she closes her eyes and turns her face to the sunshine streaming in his office window. She pictures the lush citrus orchards of Asia, where the trees droop under the weight of life-giving fruit. In her childhood, the mandarin oranges were a rare treat designed to ease winter privation and light up Christmas with sensory delights. She remembers small, eager hands peeling away the soft, smooth skin and nutrient-starved tongues savouring the rejuvenating juice. With all the will she can summon, she shuts out the surgeon's voice and the power of his malignant technology.

after the scan
in pinpoints of light
cancer's darkness

in smoker's lung
trickster cancer
wears an orange mask

CHEMO

Phony conviction. Sterile.
I need to believe
in this red-electric juice
stung into my veins,
persuade my imagination
it's elixir. My faith
in healing is real—
I've seen convincing
proofs, known mysteries of light.

I've witnessed convicts
set free, jail bars
flung open; a brightness
quickening in each cell.

I've seen the earthy shroud
left in a mound

held a burst-open chrysalis
in my palm

have prayed
and been still,
sat like a hermit
in my space,
quiet, reverent—
even my fear
convinced me of one thing: love.

And so I will see you
ruby drug
as liquid love—

trust you are spreading
the good news.

HAIRLESS

bare feet, bald head,
this is me now

losing my hair in pinchfuls,
my son and I laughing as we tug,
little firepits of wisps on the tablecloth,
patches like a newborn's
cradle cap...

even my vulva
an open orchid

Is this loss?
          or liberation?

let go of ego...be bare,
where beauty is hidden

polish the brass lamp
for radiance—

daring
          reflection

in the warm sheen
my true self:

monk,
warrior

MALEVOLENT TIDES

I spent the morning deadheading my roses. Sweat pouring down my arms in rivulets. This is what some small effort means to me.

And I smile like the little kid with the ice cream, just before he finds out his parents are divorcing. Because it could be much worse.

My liver hurts. How many times have I heard that on a Monday morning? (You did it to yourself.)

Even my oncologist, looking at a series of numbers that represent my liver enzymes, spiking off the charts, makes a crack about how much I must have been drinking on vacation. Because there's always room for blame and self-recrimination.

I'm worried, he says, and sends me for a series of right-away scans.

My liver is a manta ray: it spreads its fins to fill my torso. I didn't do it to myself. Naive as Li'l Bo-Peep, my liver did what the cancer wanted. Bulbous orbs and creeping tendrils nearly burst its straining boundaries, tumours grew faster than my organs could stretch.

And let me be clear, they may say that cancer doesn't hurt, yet they give us all the narcotics we need to bear the edge.

With my left hand, I press just below my bottom rib on my right side—a sharp pain and my stomach is strung taut like a violin, nearly hard as stone.

I still take the drug that I know isn't working. I mean, it cost my insurance $16,000 a bottle, and what if I'm wrong? I'll keep taking it until I get the results of the scan.

Shallow breath, easy pace, no, no, I'll get the next elevator.

On the scan, my lung looks collapsed. Fluid fills the sac surrounding my lungs. This invasion bulges a phantom pregnancy, a few months, if I had to guess. Something's growing inside me, at least.

I am a pillbug: I curled in protectively, as if I could somehow manufacture enough space inside my body for us both. I want to lie down and curl into myself, folding in good and bad, bitter moon and malevolent tides can wash us both away.

I wonder sometimes: how much is me and how much is it? We've been living together a long time now. Years.

I start to think, this is how I die, this is how the cancer kills me, not quickly like blowing out a candle or wishing on a star. Not over before you know its first kisses.

I die by the incremental hostile takeover of my vital organs until they no longer recall their raison d'être. It's going to pervert the intention of my very cells until they forget how to do their jobs and join up with the invaders.

A thin tube is inserted between my ribs. Two litres of cloudy liquid slowly stream from my body into plastic bottles labelled Medical Waste. Not going to die today.

A step forward, a step back. We washed my veins with Taxol for months and the tumours receded. My body shed all its hair and I was reborn.

Maybe I felt something in the dark of the night and now I need to know. Again.

OVARIAN

What do I remember of that cardinal time of life.
What some might call zodiacal: Aries, Cancer

in the balance, wanting on and on
to go...maybe, as they say, till a hundred and twenty—

The children still so young, the fluff of their favourite
flannel pyjamas in our nostrils, in our bed. I read somewhere

that inner organs glow—deep-pink and jiggly.
All except the ovaries—they're dull and grey

and pitted by release of every egg. The older the woman,
the greyer and duller the organs. But it was spring and I was

also young.
Was it that we heard a quack and found a mother duck

inside the shrub beside our driveway,
sitting on her eggs so far removed from any water—

the three of us recoiled;
she left the nest. That's what I remember from the time

before the tests. And lying in the corridor on operation day;
patients in the hall on gurneys, all of us lined up.

I remember saying that I think it's just the start.
You were standing by my side—holding the crook of my arm

till they came to take me. "You'll be in the waiting room," I said,
"that windowless cube," joking just a little for reprieve.

Your being there will make me fine, is what I didn't say—
like when you blow the candles on a cake and make a wish.

COUNTDOWN

(Italicized lines are from Nestor Zavarce's "Faltan cinco pa' las doce")

i. 1993

I am bathing a doll in a basin
        and she shows me potted cacti,
           says never to touch their red flowers.

I am cleansing her thick, rubber skin
        for her burial.

Hopscotching through families,
war and cancer sometimes stub a generation,
leave scuff marks, scatter stones among those
overgrowths   of children like the ooze of dandelions
through the pavement.
           Mother, when you sprout me,
      your first,
              you trace where the next stones will fall.

ii. 2003

A van packed like a tamarind pod,
hot scent of exhaust, gluey skin.
I am glommed in the back seat
with more children than seat belts.
When our family travels together,
our safety is only in numbers.

      Abuela Islena feels carsick.
You find her an old lunch bag:
es nada, mami, ve, no huele a nada.

I breathe kid-sweat through my sleeve,
cringe away from this vomit-prone stranger.

      Years later, you tell me
her arms nursed her fourth round
of chemo when, finally, visitors' visas

came through.
                    Better to be revolting,
to be weak,
            than not to be remembered.

iii. 2013

You have lost count of the *cincos pa' las doce*
since she died   *en una eterna navidad.*

Those tender, chromosomal gifts
left us by *esta linda viejecita* sing in us.

            Ask: will they swell like *las campanas*
            in our bodies, as in hers.

Once, I bathed a doll
            and Abuelita named the cacti
            and said never to touch their red flowers.

Once, I cleansed thick, rubber skin.

iv. 2003

Bogotá to Canada: 2 cents per minute.
The crackle as the calling card connects, then
a quavering note on the phone
                            says she has stopped.

Mother, you are far from her,

too far away to braid your fingers
            through her   ashes
                    as through hair on the head of a child
                            as her body combs into the wind.

It is a time for births and saviours,
snow-wreathed Christmas pines
and glowing, plastic mangers on the lawns.
Their blinking, artificial heat.

I ask you if she ever touched
the snow on the sierra while she lived.

In every church, you ask the men
to offer masses in her name,   call her to you,
but white-faced, white-haired strangers
glance away while kneeling in your pew.

Their bristling accents will not understand
                  the island of her name,

                                      pronounce it wrong,

            y las campanas de la iglesia están sonando,

and you shy away
from mouthing Spanish hymns
against the cold.

v. 1993

You cannot spot the freckles
that purple her hands
when you look at your own,
though their fresh root is staking
a claim on my baby-round wrists.

You fear I will not bear her gifts
with dignity, these trinkets of love
for granddaughters:

                  the sepal-hued words I won't use
            her old necklace of hard leather beads
      the imminent warp of inherited skin.

vi. 2013

This, I was not to tell you.

The smell of the women I long for
is that of the skin-warmed brass clasp
            of that necklace.

                    The string snaps
        when another girl's hands grasp
        my neck, its leather beads
        a rosary I count across the bed.

My body learns
to flourish, to bloom
like live rivers of blood.

vii. 2016

I once bathed a doll in a basin
            while Islena showed me cacti,
            said never to touch their red flowers.

                Me voy corriendo a mi casa
                a abrazar a mi mamá.

Mother, I have hidden Islena behind
other tongues, other women.
I speak her language only
to offer its taste to a lover,
and leave none for kin.

The stones that may form in my skin
withhold my will to replicate her gifts   and yours.
Faltan cinco pa' las doce   as we count
how many minutes to the first growths.

                Mother, I will not
                give you grandchildren.

Tell me how abuela lived.
How she wore lipstick
on her last day, the colour
of the sunlight on her mouth
                        betraying translation
                        to a colour I mispronounce.

Cuéntame.   Tell me
                we once bathed a doll in a basin
                and perfumed our wet, nylon hair
                with indelible salves.

DINNER THEATRE
for Sheilah

I.

I played Chopin on our grand piano,
languid legato, my mother suffering
the radiation poisoning that burned
both the noxious malignancy
and her rage.
We had lived a kitchen sink drama
in our mansion on the hill,
the setting: pure Ibsen.

I was the freak in high school that ran crying
from band practice, or French class.
Ran home to make sure my mother
was still breathing.

Is there anything I can do,
my teacher pleaded so quietly, through dense fog,
as though someone had turned a dial,
the sound down, the picture out of focus,
all kinds of dials meant to be on—
off/ off/ off.

2.

When my mother fell into a coma they
kept me from visiting her. It was melodrama now.
I had no idea what coma meant,
it was just a word after all,
and with no precedent in real life,
imagined her floating, astral travelling—
a gradation of death, (de)gradation of life into something
that wasn't life anymore.

All too soon, the porcelain teacup collection
that had quivered at her rage sat calmly,
waiting for tea to be set in the parlour.
What I remember of the shiva is a sea of tea
and every description of cake, kumquat preserves
on scones, clotted cream;
for seven days and seven nights we stuffed ourselves
with sweets, while everyone cried
and the bit players tried their best to improvise on
Is there anything I can do?

IN PASTELS

he had been strong

worked hard all of his life
never shirked from heavy loads
or responsibility

a quiet man

honourable
truthful but good at
laughing

he lies now   an
orchid

grey and white

on the hospital pillow
only a sketch

of the younger man

SONNET: NAUSEA

for NR

It's a speck lays me low: some bit of thing
my body refuses—or that refuses
my body—puts me on intimate terms
with the bathroom floor, its shiny tiles my
only horizon. There is nothing to
appease it; reduced to intake, output,
at least I'm near what I need. I have thought,
now and again, my life soured, but I
can't remember wanting this much to not
be in my body, to shuck flesh. Except
I know it will end and soon enough. For
me, if not for you, friend, what chemo
is doing to yours, making you thin and
twist. No help in wishing you better.

CLEAN MARGINS

You come to with a knot tied above your nipple,
a little lock installed atop your breast. They say that
you are mended, but now no person batters. Heart,
a hollow drum, knocks its rhythmic habit in your chest.
The room where you come to, a sterile moat, your skin
painted antiseptic pink, and in your twilight sleep, God
seems like a microbe, disinfected out of reach. *Nurse,*
you say, the word a biopsy, a test of what was taken.
Margins clean, she tells you, and you imagine remission
as the absence of opinion, a future without comment.
You will be the cleanest copy of yourself, history erased.
So how now to read the body? From your centre, sealed
with suture, what story was evicted? What character
killed off? You marshal your remainder, touch where
you are numb, taut flesh unfamiliar. You say *Nurse* again,
unaware you had already asked. Margins clean, she
repeats, this time with less kindness. The anesthetic
loosening, you grasp that -*ectomy* is the suffix form of
emptiness, a wide-open door that all your beginnings
and endings rush out of, light like garbage lifted on
an updraft, spiralling weightless toward another world.

THE IRISES

At attention
on the table, irises

hold tablets of sulphur
on their tongues. We've eaten

the bread out of the kitchen
and the eggs

have all been cracked, the little
bowls of their shells

filled with garbage.
Maybe it's true, somewhere

there are still thunderstorms,
and maybe there will be

other summers for drowning.
No one hears me say

every wall in this house
is pimpled with tumours.

No one hears me say
I know the sky is not falling.

It is lowering itself slowly
down on top of us.

COMPOST

imagine a compost heap
like the one at the back of my garden
I go there with my bucket of kitchen scraps
to toss onion skins and apple cores
passing by the purple sand cherry
my legs brushing the junipers

"visualization" is suggested
by one who loves me
because we know those who are positive
are most likely to survive
but I need to gentle an image into my being
as I lie empty under the thin green sheets
the scope winding its way inside of me
the clink of instruments the only sound
while I float above, detached
not allowing one drop of my warmth
to melt into that room

in my own bed at night
darkness is a welcome cover
the soft weight of old blankets
drapes over my hips
my husband's breathing is accented
by occasional nasal whistles
the cat pads up the stairs

one night, an image arrives
the tumour is a rotting vegetable
a hunk of yellowing cauliflower
tossed into the compost bin
surrounded by soggy peelings, dried-out flower stems
I see it wrinkle, curl inward on itself
shrivel and darken, brown then black
the tiny florets crumble apart
becoming indistinguishable from the earth

I don't tell the tumour to go, I do not command it
I don't cry it away, I can't will it away
I only think of my compost heap and the tumour
rotting away into something good for the garden
nourishing the cranesbill and lady's mantle
I planted a few years ago
so lovely at this time of year

SITES

mill road

I

spring cleaning—and in the great purge i find
a postcard marked *jeddah a.p.* and stamped
11–8–1987

almost 30 years have passed since you left
for what should have been a six-day affair
to the holy sites, calling, *i am here,*

o lord, i am here: two lengths of white cloth
as your only cover, and your peppered
hair unshorn. now, i imagine you there,

as she must have done in those months before
your return (with beard long and a slim reed
toothbrush in accordance with muhammad's

ways): circling en masse a dark, glittering cube
or passing seven times between two hills.
you must have been on your knees, then, in search

of pebbles to throw at three stone devils
which reminds me, now, *like cures like*—is that not
what homeopaths say? our world made

plausible.
                        doctrines of signatures, light.

2

today we set out to salvage what light
we can by tramping a path through late
afternoon: you, in brown socks and sandals,

your good trousers, and cotton t-shirt.
our shadows punctuate this road like breath
punctuates our bodies. because i see

your shadow fatten, tumour-like, i say, *look,
silverthorn's tree*. (one autumn we gathered
the fallen, fly-bitten pears to knock down

better fruit.) we walk, and i want to share
what i wish you had known—that love is built
not found and, like faith, cannot announce, *i*

am here, without a measure of doubt...
bread becoming what it is only through
hunger. dare i say it as we enter

your favourite dollarama and you wheel
the cart round for biscuits and bread?   yes,

one tree and a cheap store: these are the sites
to which we roam—which our feet together
sanctify before pointing us home.

SITE

for tuesdays

on tuesdays in the cramped mustard kitchen
i tear open a swab, pull the white cap
from a vial, screw tight a syringe's halves.
his sight is back—clouded lenses plucked out—
so i'm cautious as i spy the thin jut
of elbows; white shirt under which sutured
skin hides what the tumour took—a backbone
now of stainless steel, an internal cast
of rod and screws. look: he keeps an empty
chai packet stashed in his breast pocket
for the good scents of cardamom and clove.
my mouth is stern: i pretend not to love
the needle's bevelled tip, its hollow
gluttonous guzzling. neupogen funnels
like sand through a timer's slim neck. my hands
each week grow steadier than weather.
they drain the little bottle faster,
develop a square and useless pride.

the nurse mapped his skin, pointed to the sites:
abdomen (at least two inches away
from the navel); the back of the upper
arm (right or left); the thigh (never chosen).

the nurse told me to hold it like my pen.
she warned, *be swift.*
                            he kept calm, gave us nothing.

but she was not there when, at the picnic,
someone said between bites of pie,
you've had a good life, and the shade of those
five words passed over his eyes. on tuesdays
he who would never laugh or cry or tell
a joke or work all the days of my life
learns to mouth *thanks*, and *please.* that's when
i'm the closest i'll ever be to him—
both hate and love the place i enter in.

FOR ZOLI

"Dog" and "cancer" as words
  in a line may be too
    much for a poem
to bear—poems have needs
  that differ from poets',
    hate what some will call
sentiment, an excess of life
  that you, my friend, now
    face in another form.
Add "chemo," add "death,"
  and the eye turns away—
    where's room for irony?
But you are a clown
  at heart, breathing deeper
    than any poem can.

RE:CONSTRUCT

it's the hollow
thrum
on my naked
scar

the women talk:
get big boobies you've always wanted
of course you want to look like a woman
get little perky ones, you know
of course, you want balance
come on, you can do it

it's the thrumming
snake
on my hollow
chest

then the women talk:
3 lumpectomies in 3 months: fuck, just take it all
i wish now they'd taken both; i don't need them anyway
lumpectomy for me because my husband wasn't ready to lose my breast

it's the naked
hollow
on my screaming
scar

and now the women talk:
they feel like sand, and i only did it because he wanted
both of mine burst and droop like bags
necrosis
fucked mine up so bad one is an inch and a half lower;
the other hangs in my armpit. look

it's the screaming
hollow
on my naked
scar

and now the woman says:
a prosthesis is an option
look
feel
it's here
when you're ready

AND THIS IS MY FIRST TRUE SPEECH

"And this is my first true speech
And this with a decorous amplitude
And this is the middle of my life, the
Streets silent and the night covered in questions"
—Lisa Robertson, The Men

And this is my first true speech

Unprepared for the eclipse
the lines too long
Giant red telescopes offer up tiny images
I never see satellites or iridium flares anymore
I used to lie outside in the sand at four a.m.
watching bands of green light spin
We leave before the sun goes dark
My shoes walk back to the car
all of us still in shock
hangry as floating buzzards

And this with decorous amplitude

Without a script this useless holiday
Christmas no lights or tree at our house
barely the energy to wrap presents
abstract obligation
like community players in an empty theatre
we're here we have the costumes and the makeup
we know our lines and dance moves
death outlines everything
we make believe and the real
ornaments seem so ornamental

And this is the middle of my life, the

Crazy thing is cancer is in every body
cells err all the time and melt away
we sit in plastic chairs
taking notes on chemotherapy

look around at tension held in
backs and legs and hands and mouths
Flipping through the binder pages
I think we will not need this
something is happening too fast
something bad is coming

Streets silent and the night covered in questions

On my birthday they told me the votes
seven for nine against two abstentions
then another vote to defer my
exile eight books one play
twenty-five years of writing one more chance
said thirteen people with little pencils
I wonder what colour the ballots?
No more chances said four I have
two children two dogs one husband a motherinlaw
heartrage of blizzards and tigers

BAD PROFESSOR

You impose
this arbitrary reading
on a story,
faithful only
to your unique perversity
which nonetheless
with gruesome fidelity
sticks to the text
no matter how many times
one rereads it.
Perhaps time will fade
your insistent scribbles
that mar the face
of one I loved,
and mute what I learned
beneath your unseeing glare.

Original impressions,
though, set deep.
I find despite
your malignant interventions,
her tale recurs and shapes
the very language that I use,
the way I twist my face
to make my daughter laugh,
inflections in the stories
I read her before sleep.
Though your interpretation
is painfully solid,
for my child, I see,
it carries no weight: this tale I love
would always come to her
second-hand. And as she
can't know what you stole,
the story, for her, is whole.

THE VERDICT

the shuffle of feet
the rattle of a door
she comes in bringing the scent of Purell

THE HIKE

wait for your father
he is slower than you these days
uses ski poles now
takes the pressure off the knees
he says

he comes around the corner
panting

needs a rest
he says

getting old
he jokes

it no longer smells of wild rose
it no longer smells of pine

SWALLOW

she swallowed something like a great blue heron
swallowing a white jade necklace. intricate carved
birds swing in the pendulum her *tante* got
from some sailor around the turn of the century (the
last time it clicked like a purse snap shut,
like a tine clicks an empty plate). she swallowed
into the plexus the pendant lay over / beaded by
black rope. she swallowed it like her mother

swallowed the guilt for leaving
her daughter in the county tb ward
black sunken nights growth.   a guilt that blew into a tumour
lodged in the liver as she died.   a protraction
death equal to the years she ate through tubes. in rebellion
she would not eat.   all these shes are one
person   the mother the daughter the she the me the you
share guilt the guilt she
slashed into the skin of her marriage as it set
                              as she bore
it out like a child quickening
then lying still
born.

DIETHYLSTILBESTROL (DES)

after Robert Kroetsch

*from The American Heritage® Dictionary
of the English Language, 4th Edition*

- n. A synthetic nonsteroidal
  substance, $C_{18}H_{20}O_2$,
  having estrogenic
  properties and
  used...to...prevent
  miscarriage but is no
  longer prescribed for
  these cases because of
  the occurrence of
  reproductive abnormalities
  and cancers in the
  offspring of women so
  treated

*from Wiktionary, Creative Commons
Attribution/Share-Alike License*

- n. An orally-active
  synthetic nonsteroidal
  oestrogen, first
  synthesized in 1938 and
  withdrawn in the 1970s on
  being identified as a
  teratogen.

wordnik.com/words/diethylstilbestrol

DES robs
them empty
in gestation

they make no babies
change no diapers
check no homework

read no stories
pack no lunches
happy no birthdays

no graduations
no weddings
no grandchildren

childless parents
who nurture
vicariously

justify this loss
as a contribution
bestowed

upon a festering
overcrowded
planet

TECHNOLOGY

Inventors might be smug. A person
might develop new modes for seeing
where people are at any given moment.

A machine that hugs cows. That already exists.
Thanks to Temple Grandin. But nothing
that replicates being significant to others—

a glow from inside, a metaphor, a warm
hand to a chest. A closed-eye reading
of another's wants. We pine and wait.

Who are these people? Some of them
wear sweatpants and some wear lab coats
and very few smoke, but weed is edible now.

I guess we can call them dreamers, but
do we really want to? Hurry up and get
to curing all the cancers already, and also

prioritize a household machine
that makes peanut butter cups. But first
cancer, eviscerated. Every kind. Obviously.

Ugh. Bathing is complicated. Can it come in a pill?
Can everything please just come in pill form now?
I'm not even going to say please.

AT THE CORNER OF PITT AND FIRST, WHERE I LAST SPOKE TO J.P.

for J. P. Craig, 1973–2013

Never *John-Paul*, J.P., o you coyote,
goateed shaven-headed trickster
jokester, wise-cracking spliff-roller,
soberly roaming our hometown,
down to the docks tomorrow as a Merchant Marine.

Chance enough, our exchange. You're distracted.
Pitt, an outdated backdrop for you to leave,
not lean into our drink and smoke-halo
glow of years before, talks of men with men, vampires,
conspired life punctuating each debaucherous
utterance. We were responsible only to explore,
lorded over by nothing, your amused electrical
cynical eye on the longer view through the weathered
windshield of your adored Jetta.

A glance of mill-town streets,
fleeting St. Lawrence River
shimmer flat and clear at summer dawn,
onward. Such lucidity one only has passing through.

I read of your funeral years later. Surreal,
feeling a loss of vertigo of time and towns,
down, down where there is no poetry.
Reaching, mournful, my late farewell.

Keen stillborn grief, atrophied emotion dammed.
Damn it, J.P., you were taken early.
Fleeing, headlong through day, I halt with leaden limbs.
Numbly, I walk through piles of forgotten sundries,
dry dim light no guide to feet caught in languor.
You're too damn heavy in my chest. I cannot step,
kept here, never arriving where I am headed.
Speed. Gods' speed, friend.

BEFORE

The acorns are still green
and I haven't worn socks since I got here.
At home, snow has already come.
The times I stood on railway platforms

between sisters. Now, I stand
at departure gates between two homes.
I always thought I was words
and you were pictures.

Your Moleskine sketchbooks.
The snap of elastic.
I should have known you write
as well as draw with the pens

I buy you for your birthday every year.
I know you think I'll take your story.
I can't. It's yours. It's the only thing
you're taking with you.

Sitting on the shingle beach
we actually talk.
I mean, we actually listen
to each other, facing the sea.

You can't always tell what the weather is like
by looking at what people are wearing.
You told me I said that once. Pinning your socks
to the washing line, I can't remember.

Damn it, I'm a good actor.
I sit in the hairdresser's chair
and talk about my sister the artist as if you're fine.
I'm nearly as good at it as you.

Later, I sit on my own in Café Nero
on my second mug of green tea, keeping
the tea bag in for at least five minutes
so I don't waste any antioxidants.

AFTER

I wish David Bowie had died
before you. I wish he hadn't held out
for another forty-six days.
He would have shown you
it happens to everyone,
even Ziggy and Major Tom.

I played your *Hunky Dory* album
all the time when you left home.
You gave me your record player.
Until, when you came back,
you denied it and took it with you.
If I could have taken anything
back from you, it would have been
the silences on the telephone.
I shouldn't have given you those.

You told me to take away the slices
of browned apple from your bedside table,
uneaten yogourt, cold cups of tea.
You watched me measure out your morphine.
You were right not to trust anyone,
especially doctors. They didn't save you.

You don't care about the silences
on the telephone. It wasn't as if
you didn't know what I wasn't saying.

CANCER EPISODE

news of shadows—
the secretary calls
to casually report

a charm hanging
over the phone, hoping for
good results.

cancer support group—
next to the tea and cookies
a plastic breast

two surgeons
gossip; washing up to
their elbows

awake
during surgery, I control
my swearing

my surgeon
talks of his four boys;
the smoke rises

recovery room—
two nurses fight over
my gurney

confession
the margins aren't clear...
mutual forgiveness

two free bras
and a prosthesis! What
a rich country!

THESEUS & AEGEUS

Determined to be a success

and because
you lamented my life

I gathered together a book of poems
and sent it away. I always bring
my reduced, childlike self into your home.

I wonder if you know
what power I assume across the lake.

But before that white-flagged flapping "yes" could arrive,
                                    and fearing for me,
you fell down the house stairs with cancer.

CASTING CALL

No scripts, it's all
improvised, prepare
your sense of humour. Wear
sensible shoes and a silly hat. Let go
of ego, your clingy friend, know
your character won't have a lock
on suffering. The End is never
predetermined, the only absolute
mortality. The star's the tumour
the genre, a blend of slapstick
and film noir, some costumes ugly
some chic. Cocktails will be served.
Accept with dignity. Like aging
there's no immunity. The net
casts wide. The call is urgent.

SOUND CHECK

Mechanical whir of ventilation
is the voice-over of ambient dread.
Hardware and gurneys clatter
down distant corridors deep
within the bowels of suffering's mecca.
Patient hearts beat, throb and palpitate.
Oxygen gurgles, IVs alarm, bedsides
intercom. Radioactive booms
and camera zooms. Beds vibrate
to cries and whimpers
and relief sighs. Morphine drips.
Drumbeats and hallelujahs.

CLUSTER-F**K

Late one spring, my brother drowned in the folds
of an embolism that blossomed unexpectedly
as he stood by the river surveying the horizon.
The ferry was on time though we thought it early.
Next summer, my baby sister gave up the ocean
she'd just crossed. And, a month later, swimming quietly
as a goldfish, his memory just as short,
my dad kissed me one last time. Then my dog.
Six weeks later, a small leak in my vessel—
the horizon closed in, collapsing a year later
as my husband was ferried to the ICU.

RITUALS OF HAIR

(1) Preparations

She is perched on a kitchen stool, as sun splits
the back deck. An involuntary yip
escapes her throat as hair clippers lick

her temples. Hair that was hurting,
bedding for a nest. Too toxic for birds?
Her husband's hand unwavering, shadows rise.

(2) Buying the wig

Limp as a dead guinea pig, a wig
nests in a cardboard casket
swaddled in folds of tissue.

Fine as fishnet stockings, a woven cap
scoops the globe of her head,
a plastic buoy of synthetic hair is anchored.

Why this ritual? Why the cover? She stares
in the mirror, hands cover breasts, bush—
she has neither, naked, every limb, crook,

a drowning rat swept along the gutter,
clutching at any branch or rock: Nature shakes

her loose until shame is a newborn calf
lost amongst the legs of her maternal clan.
Trunks swing, we listen with our feet for home.

(3) Reciprocity

He is perched on a kitchen stool, as summer sun
splits again. Clippers in hand, her husband's head
bowed. Unwavering, burnished steel blades
cross his scalp. Poised as a Buddhist monk.

RESCUE DOG

You came to us
around the time I was healing.
That windy chemo spring
when I pulled out my hair
in fistfuls and it flew away
to line the nests of birds.
Hope snapped in the air
like prayer flags.

As I was losing my hair
in came yours: dark, abundant,
soft for petting.
Velcroed to sofas and carpets.
Helpmate. Canine healer. You,
the shaggy blackboard
we scrawled our wishes on.

SHATTERED CITY

Auntie took the ivory vase from the old funeral home—a universe of cities carved into its husk. Her hand read those needle pricks like Braille. Father, she thinks, considering what a serious man you were, you manage to look like cartoon coyote in a funeral suit, when painted. Your mischievous smirk lit my fire from its frame in the hallway. Stole the key to the cabinet while the new funeral directors went at the freshly laid-out bodies—bees to honey. Mother's cabinet. Her artifacts, gathered in times before her womb shot out too many children, before her fingers became twisted trees putting shells on every basket and mirror frame that passed through the condo at Park Place, she thought. Auntie's slippery hands did the deed. What did it matter anyhow? she thought. When you have a breast carved off of you, collecting what is rightfully yours takes hold like a prosthetic.

*

She shouldn't be getting this right now—the incision hasn't healed enough yet. Tell her that. Look, lady. I get it, if you haven't noticed, I have no leg, ya know? I get it. Diabetes took the leg. Ivy tattooed. Their yelling has stopped, I have passed Auntie an iced tea from the corner store and Percy is being more gentle with the needle, thank Christ. Inky ivy grows across her incision while she sips the drink. Ivy inking its way across a destroyed chest, wound its way around arms, found navel.

*

Auntie left me a shattered city. Passing shattered city. Passing Polish amber on a chain. If you were lucky enough to be here when her house cleared out, you got the real pieces. Anchored in my family's houses: the babushka doll from her kitchen, Salish paintings from the coast, the antique stool from her treatment room. Shhh, don't say anything. I will pass your city. I have it in my basement that vase, but it's broken. She would have wanted you to have more than a tin of buttons.

THE QUEEN OF SURGICAL RECOVERY

Resplendent
in early October sun
lying on the front step of
Mount Sinai
bare from the waist up
her lush breasts
witnesses
to medical professionals
scurrying on University Ave.
The silent sun maintains her
she will heal
or die
on her own terms. Transforming like a burnt-
out star divides itself into
carbon atoms and building blocks
of the universe.

THE UNDERSIDE OF THE LINE: EIGHT CANCER (FATHER) POEMS;

"Better a semi-colon than a full stop." —*John Lavery*

;

a threat of where the body breaks. I tell him, slowly. parthenogenesis, without benefit. retract the soul of divine beings. pour boiling water. a narrow, furrows. we will begin to need to know. cross out the nexus, pretend it is only line.

;

what can he say? he says. cancer blossoms, polyps pulp, a sequence. enact a restless word, pursuit. medieval skin, unforms. a uniform attention. what groundswell, fertile. bulbs. doctor says, we dig that up.

;

plough, the side of body. plenty, blowing horns. upon reflection, points to his desk. marks what gives impression of. gravity. my own same sleeping self. what few, to calm. the telephone rings. his many friends. stillness, calms.

;

mercury, the basement. shatters. biographical ascent. the cistern rattles, cobwebs. well the well was well enough, is good. submit your pictures of an hour. direction of a narrow channel. small or just as small. a honeymoon. grace, period. the furnace restart button hold, you hold, three seconds. undertow.

;

exceptional days. we daydream. this century-house. exhales, his seven decades. pictures invite the past, a truly foreign land. something to do with snow, the thaw. dream a silent movie, dawn. remarkable, reading. some other kinds of birds.

;

radio, shores St. Lawrence. swims upstream. rain seeks its level, lake. in our uncertainties, comfort.

;

it goes on, hummingbirds. underside of the line. rarely a word but many.
alphabets absorb their birth, umbilical. fifty-two playing cards with only
missing, one. my sister's boy in living room, cartoons. a church mouse.

;

breadbox, caustic nerve. turn of weather changes. cautionary. prepares but not
presumes the worst. we have his chequebook. know where the wills.

SOLDIER

You fought in a war against
an enemy stationed in your own body.

You negotiated with
chemotherapy, morphine.
Even tried herbs,
sucked grapes
baptized in holy water.
A pilgrimage to the local cathedral.
Your lips touched
the bishop's hand.

Tumours still invaded your skin.
You drank
from the goblet of death.

In a vineyard in the Beqaa Valley
spoiled wine dripped
from a barrel of crushed grapes
into your dark blue veins.

BEDSIDE SERVICE

My father hits his chrome bell
over and over. My mother answers
with a groan, leaves me listening
to her leather slippers shuffle
down the tiled hall to where he lies,
open-mouthed. Only she's allowed
to nurse his brittle body. I retreat
into the kitchen, listen for her return.
Nothing's to be read in teacups.

Against the window screen, a moth
flutters my disquiet. At a bedside,
a chrome bell. The night

has an easy breathing. I'm ready to dip
into delusion, escape outside
before this house implodes.

YOU ARE HERE

As I walk my neighbourhood streets,
unaware I'm in need of direction,
the map addresses me boldly: YOU ARE HERE!
I consider the arrow that points
to a snake of paths.
Houses along the way marked
as little dark boxes.

And now, light and bright,
another small box
with the welcoming smile of a facilitator
and a hopeful semicircle of chairs.
I sit beside you, follow the PowerPoint: prognosis, radiation therapy,
androgen therapy, prostatectomy... Glass walls
show me an unstained sky
while knowledge grows in me the way mistletoe
invades a tree, takes hold.
No, not *here.*
I have not a shred of interest
in being *here.*

I want my place beside you, my head on your chest,
my fingers tracing ribbons on your skin.
Your breath deep and slow, eyes closed.
When I lift my face, look up, sure enough
there's a big golden arrow pointing to us.
You Are Here.

ONCOLOGY DEPARTMENT AT TRILLIUM HOSPITAL

A young woman sits in the waiting room.
Leafs through *Glamour* and *Time.*

I don't know her exact diagnosis,
but she is wearing a chemo scarf.

She's sipping on a pastel pink straw
from a supersized Styrofoam
cup, of what can only be prep solution.

If you could just change the backdrop,
you would swear she's at McDonald's.

Fast food. Check!
Chemical preservatives. Check!
Formaldehyde leaching from plastic
packaging; GMOs. Check!

It all makes me think of Jesus,
at the Last Supper,
and the way he was betrayed.

The scourging. The thorns. The nails.
The bitter vinegar they offered him
on a sponge in his final hour.

The story of his murder neatly staged,
retold in twelve sequential stations. Process
of prognosis after diagnosis and then the step-
by-step theatrical stage, set.

As if always, after the breaking of the bread,
a handing over for anointing follows
in a ritual of scientific protocol.

And we comply. That's all we can do.
Ticking each step off on the clipboard,
completing every step to our undoing.

LONGING

If there are no fish-houses; no
secrets worth spilling; no mad,
filthy serenades, what, then
to speak of? Birds
picking the last seeds, drains
pulling water into the sewers. Your car,
in storage, tucked up to sleep
in a stranger's barn.

This year, too many deaths.
And by "this year," of course,
I mean all. Is it worse
to miss you, or not? Even a small
hiatus in longing means you've moved,
gone further off.

So when on a summer night I find myself
at the lakeshore, hunched and wailing
in a phone booth, then...thanks
to whoever arranges these things.
For a moment, you're here.

STAY

Are you there? Is that you?
You've been gone, or I have
so long I've forgotten
your voice. My voice. Stay
this time, please. At least
long enough for coffee.

BELLYFLOP

I'm young, and haven't had my babies yet, so I'm unburdened by mother eyes, mother love. I'm tall, wearing baggy floral capris held up to my armpits by red suspenders. Pink ballet flats, and empty frames from a pair of square tortoiseshell glasses my grandma wore the decade I was born. A soft pink chiffon blouse, a red beret with a silk rose pinned to the front. Overly rouged cheeks, and a red nose.

She is tiny, hairless, wearing a banana Metamucil hospital gown over her small bones and polar fleece pyjama pants, too big now, even though they're only age eighteen to twenty-four months, with sallow skin and a smile larger than she can carry. She is maybe three, and will be kept as comfortable as possible until she stops breathing.

We see each other down the hospital hallway connecting Starbucks and Shoppers Drug Mart, filled with fast-moving civilians drinking coffee and trying to get somewhere. Time slows, and stops, along with the movement in the hall, and we are lying on the freeway floor side by side, grinning at each other. She takes my face in her hands and pulls it right up close to hers so our noses are touching and shows me the insides of her eyeballs and self.

When we get up she hugs me, holds on to me, arms around my waist and face against my belly like I'm a tree trunk and she's trying not to get blown away by the breeze that is making her little legs shake under their twenty-five pounds of daily diminishing weight. She climbs me like a playground. We wordlessly dance the maypole around each other. She jumps into this moment with absolute abandon and complete commitment, like a bellyflop into a summer pool, pulling me with her, and our laughter is the splash as we land.

Her parents watch from the sidelines, along with her grandparents and gathered friends who have collected and follow her like a flock of nervous baby ducks. She has only today in her eyes, but they are seeing all their tomorrows without her. Although she is the one who won't be around much longer, they are the ones who are dying.

TOOK YOU IN PIECES

1)

It took your voice,
your trachea an open pit

"I cannot speak..."

The cylinder pressed under your jaw
producing grey vibrations, robotic
monotones
of "B" science fiction

"...but I will live!"

I never doubted it.

2)

It took your taste,
a pipe penetrating your belly
into which beige, life-sustaining liquid
was pumped

The same syringe
sprayed me as I read in the yard, rain
dropping from a cloudless sky,
turning to see you chuckle.

3)

It took your...

you know the rest.

DREAMS I HAD THE WEEK BEFORE MY GRANDMOTHER PASSED AWAY

The House Dream:

I dream my grandmother is a house. First, she is the various apartments of her childhood: the boarding houses and tiny one-bedrooms in the Bronx, Coney Island, Brighton Beach. Then, she is the flat in the Red Hook housing projects she and Morty live in as newlyweds (she is nineteen), then the fifteen years they spent at the Sheepshead Nostrand Houses, and (finally) I dream that my grandmother is the final destination of her and Morty's climb into the middle class: 53-44 Bell Boulevard, Bayside, Queens. On the map the house is boxed in by highways, service roads, ocean. It is a house full of boys, then a house full of men; a house of argument, of protest, of political hope and political despair; a house of grief; a house of grandchildren visiting from Philadelphia, from Toronto. An attic of memories, a basement of sloshing sorrow.

The City Dream:

I'm a child with the eyes and fears of an adult and she is a dark-skinned woman with the heart of a careening bird, the kind that stays airborne for months at a time. The two of us emerge from the deep darkness of the subway into bright Manhattan. The buildings are dream-large, they are impossibly large. We sit on a bench in a small green park, the city an intricate machine all around us that, thanks to the dream-time, we instinctively know—skyscrapers so tall and yet still this brightness—and she tells me stories of being a secular Jewish radical in the second half of the twentieth century.

The Mirror Dream:

Help! Morty's been dead for thirty years! Thirty years! And Paul, poor Paul, my first child, gone at forty-one. *Help!* We grew up on the beach, ate eggs we fried in the sand— *Help!* she calls, and we don't know whether to laugh or avert our eyes.

The Story Dream:

Have I ever told you how we met? she says. A mutual friend introduced us at a Young Communists meeting. Have I ever told you how we met? He was doing work on my house, and we struck up a friendship. Then that incident happened with that lady and they threw him in prison for fifteen years. Oh, did that judge have it out for Puerto Ricans! I visited him, oh yes. And now we live together. I am a bridge. My son died before his time. My first of three boys. I quit smoking some years after that, though at times I crave it like I crave rye bread, like I crave sanity and compassion in our elected officials. We eat mun cookies and laugh at the latest world war. In the Arctic we would chip ice into our glasses right from the glacier, she says.

The Elevator Dream:

I'm in a small Southern Ontario city looking at apartments. I have a cup of ice that I am chewing on. We go up the elevators, see the apartments, go down the elevators. I keep chewing the ice, which isn't depleting.

Now we are driving along country roads in the middle of the night, the news of the death fresh as the cool Georgian Bay air. We drive through tall trees, past secret lakes, under condemned bridges, puddles of darkness that the headlights cannot or will not reach pooling at every dip in the road.

Now I'm standing on the Brooklyn Bridge. I am alone. The city is going backwards and forwards in time. From trees to skyscrapers to trees, Wall Street to wall, Canal to canal, pre-contact to seventies dilapidation. I'm worried the bridge itself will disappear, that the city will fragment, the rebar of subways melt into non-existence. But for now it holds. I have a decision to make: to cross into the city or head for the outer boroughs, the island that eventually ends in a sharp nub of sand and rock. I wait. The sun sets.

I continue to wait.

The Procession Dream:

There's a lineup to the coffin. Each person puts one item: the keys to her house; dried wildflowers; the yellow-and-red "IMPEACH" sign that had been forgotten in the attic for decades; the collected Alice Munro; the collected Pete Seeger; playbills from a lifetime of playbills; a piece of stone chiselled from the Brooklyn Bridge; a photo of her grandchildren; hair rollers; a pack of Parliaments; a bottle of Clinique Aromatic Elixir; a box of Peace Calendars; a box of Bev Doolittle calendars, birthdays and plays and doctor appointments and poetry classes written in her fine scrawl; rye bread; mun cookies; Zabar's dark roast coffee beans; coffee cake; a gallon of NYC water, the best tap water in the world; an assortment of New York cheeses; another rye bread; the desk she and Morty shared, where he spent nights studying for his PhD thesis on reforming adult education, where she marked homework, where they tried, in their own, small way, to do something.

The Window Dream:

I was at my desk, I think, I was at some sort of desk, and I was typing. I typed: "Her name was Frances Kreuter. She knew the name of every wildflower. The men in her life all had bad hearts. She married Morty in the basement of a shul on Ocean Parkway. She was involved in establishing the first New York City teachers' union. She fought against racism, classism, and homophobia her entire life. When she'd cross the border and visit us in Toronto she would always bring gifts from her travels, an American fifty-dollar bill for each of us, gleefully exchanged for Canadian dollars, sometimes doubled in value. She died still fighting." I stop writing and look out the window. A giant bird is soaring through the sky. Seeing the bird makes me realize I was dreaming: it was much too big, much too high, for it to be anything but a dream. I think about this for a moment, decide it doesn't matter. I go back to the work.

"She knew the name of every wildflower," I type.

THE NEW HANDSHAKE

They all ask. She
is surprised, not since her teens
have her breasts been so
irresistible. So, she begins
calling it "the new handshake."

They all start with the usual
pleasantries—name, position—then
chat for a moment or two, but
the question always follows—
"May I examine *the, ugh, breast?*"
She has no idea what
they would do should she
answer "no." Does not see this
as an option.

At first this was handled formally—
a gown offered, then a moment
or two alone. But as the numbers
of instances grew, she
became inured to the ritual—
unbuttoned, dropped a strap, served it
up to whomever asked.

After the fifth
go-round, she began keeping count
(adding her own set of rules—
tallying only *new* requests). By
radiation session #30, two dozen
different hands had touched, squeezed,
palpated her.

Seeing her GP for the first
time post-treatment, she asks, "Do you
want to examine it?" Is surprised
by his blush, his question: "Why
would I?" Laughs as she replies, "Well,
everyone else does. I wouldn't want
you to feel left out!"

CLUB TOXIC

She stands in line
beside her husband. A young man
(is he the patient or the "plus one"
they've been told to bring?)
points to the man at the door,
clipboard in hand. "Like at a dance club,"
he offers. Some of those waiting
in the mandatory Pre-chemo Seminar line
chuckle. An older woman pipes up, "Son,
no one wants to be on the list for *this club*!"

And, of course, this is true. No one
wants to hear that soon they will be *toxic*—
the clothes they wear put in a separate
laundry bag, washed—not once but twice—
in a segregated load. That after using the toilet
they must close the lid and flush, then flush again.
That the dishes they use must be washed,
then re-washed just to be sure.

From somewhere in the back,
a woman asks about sex and the room
comes alive with the kind of titters
usually reserved for a middle school
sex-ed. class. Nonplussed, the nurse
answers, warning that every precaution
should be used—condoms, dental
dams, surgical gloves.

She begins to laugh, tears
running down her cheeks, and
the laughter spreads. One woman shouts,
"This ain't happenin'," and the members
of Club Toxic clap wildly, united
for the moment
in the absurdity of it all.

SHOES

1.

This grief is too big for me,
a pair of shoes that just doesn't fit right.
I wander, galumph around in this feeling all day.
And by evening I lie down in the cool
white bed, entire body aching, including those thin
hidden muscles I don't know the names of.

Why do I walk for hours? I am looking for you,
for the calm spread of forehead,
easy stance—but you are not here.
I search for you in cities you've never seen
and in halls where strangers' voices ring and rise
but no one says your name, and nothing means meaning.

It is like trying to find a season
that ended weeks ago. Where blue morning glories
grasped the fence along the park, fingers of leaves hook wire:
their edges gold-brown, dry-whispering. I come home
and go out again. Sky ridged grey. From the clouds
leaves shoot like bright cinders from a fire.

2.

Stretch marks: my body tired of holding everything.
Baby, bottle, reusable mug, stroller, telephone. Don't drip,
don't drop. A disembodied voice scraping through static,
half-words. Low-charge. Blanks, blips, whispers. Still wondering
what you tried to say. A network that sways like tree branches.
Our final conversation already you were far away.

A quiet song, cancer fumbles across the body,
then goes forte, pressing down on all parts. There's no good
way to die, people tell us. We struggle to say *lymphoma*,
only having held the diagnosis in our mouths for ten days.
I fold away clothes we can't wear again, the baby's shorts, tanks.
He's learned five words since you...left. I've learned

to speak in past tense. Your own clothes still suspended
in a smoke-thick closet. Grey ghost wool of you.
Beige corduroy. Permanent Certs of chest pockets. This predictable
mint, half-wrapped, lingering, flavoured with a memory of arms
toned and tanned, the power in them and
this scent on your living, speaking breath.

Please let me forget: how your chest waned, moonlike,
slivered ribs. Your feet, edema-dark, swelled two sizes
while the rest diminished. Your teeth yellowed. No one
should know how your mind got lost. How gums receded, how
the bones' calcium seeped into bloodstream. Your body ate you
as you sat in the brown chair making funny faces at the baby.

3.

It's been two seasons now and you are unpacked up,
like someone who has gone on a trip but left everything
behind. I imagine you driving, hands on wheel,
inside one of the cars I pass on these matted freeways.
Casually glancing into rear-view. The only afterlife
I'll believe in. Why not imagine you heading east?

Sun paints pavement white. I could picture you
in a sudden life elsewhere. A better heaven
than the dark—but the dark, the dark has its songs.
I've started to think that right and wrong
are the same flavour, like coffee with cream stirred in.
After all, there's no reason to death.

At home your things wait for you to come back,
reanimate them: the comb, file, nail clippers, razor
and squeeze bottle of grocery-store aftershave.
The oversized new shoes on a now-dusty floor
keep your shape—round toes, slightly wrinkled
tongues, as if you've only just stepped out of them.

GREATER THAN AND LESSER THAN

When you have eaten all you can,
two spoons worth of pudding or applesauce,
I'll kiss you on both cheeks. Every day
until you have no cheeks, until
the cheeks sink into the skull, and hope
sinks too. Until you fold
your hands, lie down, lie still now,
as the smoke rings of old cigarettes dissipate,
a chalk alphabet washed out of the air.

Until you can only whisper. Then I'll go—
no more to be done—drive through the day.
In the night a tall glass of Guinness
appears, poured before me, the darkness
filling up. Your last words to me were not
Don't go, but *Take me with you.*

I feed the baby, but cannot eat. I hold
the phone while sleeping. Sleep it will;
little words like *yes* and *no* too heavy for you now.
The only call to come, the one I can't face.
How many times will I remember this voice
that flashes and fades like a shadow on the wall?
Waiting is an arithmetic that consumes us.
Greater than and lesser than. A symbol
on which children draw teeth.

UPON HEARING OF ANOTHER CELEBRITY DEATH BY CANCER

The truth is I think of my own father
dead at 59, I think of myself
fatherless; my dad dying and dying
I think: I hope that's not cancer, that _____.
My whole life my dad has been vanishing,
lost (*sing it*) to the great by and by—
I exaggerate; there were those 14
years when I was a girl & Dad was well.
Plus there were the 40 years before then
nearly impossible to imagine.
The thought of it, my father as a child,
his parents as strange to him as mine to me—
My dad got into the war and fistfights,
afterwards he got into more whisky,
then my dad got into sports radio.
He was at the top of his game when he died.

My father, a minor celebrity
himself, packed the house at his funeral mass.

SUITE

1.

Brief

Carry lymphoma around in a box,
expiry date smudged.
Suddenly want to push
all the flowers together
(who used to boast
of looking well at one).

I

Raise the bamboo blind,
the long day completely bright,
my life
dripping to the sea.

2.

Push back

A year later and it's finally processed. Now to make
art out of vomit and fear. The first reaction
too in the bone (its marrow—dry, dysfunctional—
hears the blood's death-speak). Why
pretend, debate—the long dying, the short, the merits of?
You can never have too much life until you can.

Submitting to "18 months to 4 years" pushes you.
Books to be written, trips to take.
Noting on calendar: dead by April?
dead by November? mind clears.

3.

Rock

I think: submission should be enough,
but no, released from chemical misery,
in remission, I pump my fist at sky,
nothing solid except this rock
I come to sit on, scrape snow off. I say:
it will be dry tomorrow, lichen visible.

To get here I trudge miles through melting snow.
Which boots? The ones that hold my feet together
or those that keep them dry? Lovely,
I say, lovely to choose, sit stay.

4.

Portal

I haven't mentioned my portacath.
(Don't know if it's one word in my chest
or two. That doesn't matter.)
It's a passageway, a wire through skin to heart's blood,
where pumps the protocol: saline, chemo, immunotherapy,
cortisone to calm it all down, the last dose.

Here's a joke I didn't get till hours later at home.
In my ignorance asked the chemo nurse how long
a portacath lasts. "I once," she said, "knew one to last
eight years." Her pause, closed look at my face.

5.

Waving

Get these poems out of me! Though pots wait
to be scrubbed, garbage sorted.
Go through all my stuff. Paper napkins:
don't need those, use them up. Thirty mugs!
Give away. Get rid of dust, polish surfaces,
make space, work. Get these poems out.

Sugar no long necessary. But salt—
salt has become tongue's delight.
A small pile in my palm to be finger-dipped, licked.
Haven't done that since I was a child.

6.

Drowning

This is no rehearsal   no small internal adjustment
to be made to gut   or a reaming of the heart—
the throat to groin split   this   this my friends
is it   rescued today   and I'm shining when I can

Imagine an upside-down life   you walk on your head—
your feet smile and nod at the others   your arms drag
alongside your head   your head gets sore but you keep smiling
through your toes   mumble   shout   mud getting in mouth
offer sadness   yes
and   I mean to say   joy

7.

Today

Oh wise the woman walking in the sun,
fragments sequenced—the walk, the sun—
her hat and gloves discarded as she warms.
Snow-lined fields, colours in the house perplex.
She lays her gaze down onto patterned wool,
asphalt. Don't be fooled, she says.

This is not the best but it is close,
and she will die but not today—tomorrow.
The sun on her face, in her eyes, the walk in her body,
pull together in this last line.

A POEM ABOUT THE PANCREAS

Even if you opened a practice on Harley Street
no patient would come in with complaints
about his pancreas:
"I think it's my pancreas, Doc!"
—unless they too are a fellow professional
also educated
out of their natural mind;
few patients will be alarmed by the word,
not like the "heart,"
a word that summons the feeling "the biscuit"
in the best of us.

Years from now
when you trundle in
thin and yellow, depressed
for abdominal films,
you too will have forgotten

your pancreas; and the news "It's cancer
of the pancreas" will hit
like an old family secret you knew all along;
"I'm sorry, but it's cancer
of the sweetbread."
"Not the sweetbread!"—"Yes,
and, with proper medical management
early surgery
and a very rigid diet
you can look forward to at least
three months."
When the pancreas goes,
it goes.

Not even the diabetic
whom the pancreas
torments by degrees
can help us conceive
of that familiar; even a poet
is at a loss for metaphor;

nothing short of a surgical exploration
will unearth

the thick spongy worm
twisted twice on itself
buried deep in the viscera
silent behind its curtain of peritoneum,
with a head, a body
and a tail,
using the man's face.

BREAKAWAY

The Cliftons loaned me a rusty stake
to dislodge a breakaway piece of bog from my shore,
but it's a toothpick against this stinking tonnage.
Aware of my age and city-slicker status,
Mrs. Clifton, who winters here, offers,
"Call Frank. *He'll* know how to move it along."

Frank arrives in a pickup.
Paunchy, balding,
five years my junior,

but he's weathered as a petroglyph,
and has a helper, a beanpole teenager
already ruddy in the face.

"Ya got t'git the water *underneath*
and let her do the liftin',
like one of them glaciers
that carved out one of them canyons
—-not much speed, but plenty o' power.

That's their technique,
and in ten minutes the little island

is heading back into the lake
toward someone else's frontage.

"What do I owe ya?"
"Twenty.
Put your docks in fer fifteen more."

"So, you're as good at lodging things
as getting them to move?"

"Pardon?"

"Okay, you guys do the docks.
I got a big patch of field to mow."

He eyeballs it.
"Fifty, and that's done too.
Buddy here rides a mean mower.
Don't ya, Buddy?"
Let's see: Fifty dollars
+ a twelve-pack of appreciation
= peace of mind.
More time to write, to swim...

City mouse, country mouse.
city louse, country grouse.

"It's a deal."

Before they start on the lawn,
Frank takes me aside:
"Mrs. Clifton says you're a doctor.
You know anything about
that whole *stagin'* business,
you know, Stage I, Stage II...?

"A bit..."

"The wife has a Stage III
and it don't look good."

"What's the, er, primary, um,
where did it start?"
"Bowel, large bowel,
but some of it must've broke off,
'cause now it's in
her bones."

"Oh. I'm so sorry.
How is she handling it?"

He narrows his eyes,
"What kind o' medicine you do?"

"Psychiatry—"

He removes his baseball cap,
wipes the sweat from his brow,
pushes back a crest of greying hair,
winks at Buddy.
"That'll pay the bills..."

OPEN CITY

A student from years ago makes a beeline for me
as I sit in the hospital cafeteria prescribing poems, the sickness flying.
She says she's been trying to get here for months. *I'm in chemotherapy.*
I use its full name 'cause I don't want to get intimate with chemo.

I have no idea who she is. Her soft face gets softer.
She holds the poems, and crumples with delight.
No wonder I didn't recognize you. This is what no protection looks like.

I don't wear a mask but I've had a flu shot.
It's the white coat I love the most.
One day I'll declare armistice with my body.

MASS

And now she has a mass
in her stomach.
I get off the phone and feel
a gathering in my own.
There is no singing or praying,
just tension, a gathering
dark if I could see inside, which I can't,
the body not being transparent.
I can feel it pull together
a huddle, a crowd—
not religious but convicted.
Or not yet convicted
but charged,
charged with being.

PING

to my local access network of time
where my father lies medically jet-lagged
& my drowned spaniel curls at my belly

ping

to when dad fell out of the car
his frail body faded yellow
his voice weak & moaning

ping

to hearing him from my blue bedroom
unable to keep myself from gazing
into a shining stack of comic books

ping

to turning away & walking
from his coffin into the sunshine
& all the gloomy, worried faces

ping

to a sparkling hospital playroom
playing with bubbles while doctors
cut a cancer off my sister's leg

ping

to a drunken punch-up in Munich

ping

to our miscarried child
to our first born purple
& yelling from far away

ping

to six years later when he learned
that bears can stand up

NOT LIKE ON TV

Are you ready?
That's what Supportive Friend is meant to ask. Big breath from protagonist who emanates inner strength through sparkly eyes as air crackles with extraordinariness. A slight nod. Clippers buzz while Supportive Friend shaves off a first strip of hair. Music swells.

That's what's supposed to happen.
Instead:

Can I give you a mohawk?
Supportive Friend asks.

I consider this. It would be a funny photo op, like a kiss from a sea lion at a marine park. Nope. Not in the mood. I put away the clippers and ask for a Mia Farrow pixie cut—hope for the best. The cut gets me through Christmas. By February I look like a baby orangutan: sparse orange hairs waving above a scalp horizon. By May I've lost my eyebrows too. When I draw them on, they keep disappearing. People on the street can tell I'm sick now. When I catch them staring, they look away—they've had nightmares about being me. I start to feel most comfortable at the hospital where everyone either looks like me, or is caring for someone who does. I finish chemo and my hair begins to grow back.

That's when I decide to shave my head.
I want a fresh start—a clean pate.

Are you ready?
Supportive Friend asks.

We choose the 3 mm blade. The resulting buzz cut doesn't look good on me, but it *feels* good—very soft. I discover my head is a little lumpy, and on the back, there's a wine-coloured birthmark I've never seen.

Stork bite,
says my GP.
It looks like Madagascar,
says my oncologist.
Maybe you can go there when you get better.

NURSING HER HOME

Old women with soft palms folded in
laps unused to lavender stillness wait,
    fingering the pseudo silk of a blouse
frayed beyond repair. Wait forever
    to pick them up on eternity's date.

Wait for the next meal the orderly wheels
    you meanwhile round to table. Wait to
      greet a nurse in whose face you recognize
    a cousin dead half a century revived for
lunch. Wait for nursing to commence.

Wait for home to return. The one promised,
the old one half remembered, half dreamed:
    a flushed garden of poppies, peonies, lupin
and cardinals along flashing scarlet spectrum
    in lush, flagrant harmonics of house wren.

Pink scalp shines through white wisps as if
sun-touched. What, who is pulling your hair?
    Pulling your mind beyond the present, back
    forward or out of the brain cave into the new
light that blinds your blinking rheumy eye.

The photo on your door is there to remind staff
    you once were a person, a bright war bride,
even though name tags are misplaced and you
    wear someone else's worn slippers. You, once
so fastidious, don't notice now, don't care.

The elevator only descends from this locked
ward. Windows allow in light but not air.
Here they consider you safe, your needs met.
    For the first time ever, you own time, despite
rigid routine. Wander free where you can.

Wait in the hall for the upcoming call. Wait
in your patient wheelchair for the next round.
    Wait while the cancer that hollowed your bone cage
       grips you one last time. The handshake of a friend
     at last offers you ease, a reprieve now, an end.

RIGHT HERE

He lowers himself into the deep armchair
His feet in leather slippers pull over a stool
Forgive me. It's more comfortable with them up

Through the tracksuit, his legs lie toothpick-thin
His face, clean-shaven, unlined, not too pale
I still have my hair; that's a surprise

The cell offers a desk and laptop, a kitchenette and toilet
A flat-screen TV, a CD player, plus his stack of favourites
I have everything I need, right here

Potted violets, azaleas with merry cards line the sill
His single bed (made) stands in an alcove with no window
I don't even mind if it rains

A bandage covers the gash on his head from a faint
Blue, clear eyes widen, childlike
I think I'll make it, don't you?

WHAT BOUT YOU?

Who dead?
Mama dead.
What kill her?
Big C.
Which part?
In her lung.

But after me
never see
your mama
suck a cigarette
no time in her life?

True word
but Papa smoke
all two pack a day
when time bad.

So how your papa?
Dead too.
What kill him?
Big C.
Which part?
All part—

spread so till
at the last
it stay like
embroidery
round him neck
bung him throat.

Poor man couldn't
swallow little rum
to take him
through.

So how
your bredren,
your sistren stay?

Big C catch them too.
Two prostate, one colon,
one breast, one lung,
one ovary.

Lord, girl! How
God could play so bad
with all of unoo?

So tell me...
What bout you?

BOUNCE

Enough of the bully
in the mirror

The dense dermal choreography
and jagged skate of the scalpel
dragged across my chest are clear
the remains
of a semaphore signal
dodged
Last night I dreamt of my scar
Today I smash the mirror and pivot
half cleaved
sans seriffed
and signatured

My inventory is affirmed
there's just one
It's enough

TRANSPORTED

Every morning she swallowed three pills
with a glass of water while sitting up in bed. Every Monday
she walked into a clinic where they extracted three
teaspoons of blood into slender tubes. Her blood was the colour
of pomegranate guts, of a woodpecker's bright crest plunging
through pine-scented forest. Sometimes
she would wait in a room with other faces until she heard
her name. At the end of each clinic day she would stare at a
backlit screen at home and watch numbers swim
past. The numbers were free-floating in her blood
like tadpoles newly burst from their jellied egg mass.
They were also free-floating on her screen, thanks to the dark art
of information theory and transport.

It was all very abstract. Until the morning she swallowed
three numbers with a glass of pomegranate guts while sitting
in a backlit forest. Faces swam past in slender tubes. She ate eggs
with jelly straight off the teaspoon as she waited to be
transported through the dark arts. Information is
made of glass. Should it plunge into your free-floating
home it can never be extracted. But you will know the scent of blood
the colour of pine, the brightness of water, the clinical difference
between a woodpecker's stare and a burst
screen. In a room of abstractions
every theory wears a pillbox hat. She took her bed for a walk.
At the end she heard three tadpoles call her name.

NOT AGAIN

My mother decades ago,
My brother-in-law a few years ago.
You would think I would be an old hand at this.

I read the obits with a wary eye.
I look for the code words:
Courageous battle.
Before her time.
Thanks to ALL the staff.

They all tell the same story:
A brutal, exhausting marathon to the finish line.

Yours hits close to the bone.
Extended family this time,
My cousin's partner,
We huddled and talked about our cancers,
Both very different but ultimately the same.
Neither of us granted
The grace of a cure.
We each swore we would learn to live
With these monkeys on our backs,
Determined our lives would not be defined by our cancers.

But your cancer did define your life,
It moved to your bones and then your liver.
Your body abandoned you
Long before you were ready to abandon life.

Will I be another one?
How will they tell my cancer story?

Courage, one of your friends
Whispered to me as I left your wake.

HEAT ADVISORY

When my parents attended my graduation,
there was no air conditioning.

Hundreds packed into a temporary tent
just east of the Osgoode Hall Law School.

My father was 70 at the time, my mother, 61.
They drank bottled water.

As he aged, my father got more ill-tempered,
but one can forgive him, for that at least,

after four heart attacks, two strokes, diabetes.
It took cancer to end him, end his journey.

It was his God-given right to complain.
Crankiness was his lifestyle; it defined him.

At my brother's wedding the music was loud,
and my father, 69 at the time, complained.

Nothing was done and he had had enough; he left.
We did not recognize his pain.

He took public transit home.

NO ROOM FOR GLOOM

"Hope
that thing with feathers"
—Emily Dickinson

It's easier to be buoyant
when no stage is tolled
        say   that dreaded four
signifying the spread

divisive cells scouting the body
for congenial settlements
to colonize and kill

Soon Sudbury's oncologists
will lay out the map
to chemo or not your colon
when to light-burn your lungs

tiny operable tumours
one-way ticket to hope
no room for gloom

Who knows how when or if
the tipping point arrives
Sorry   no space at the inn
no more defences mustered

or—maybe the heart takes
a hike   blood and nerves
suddenly anti-social

Whatever   pray hope   I
keep seeding the feeder
hosing the birdbath
colonizing joy

BEER ON THE ROOF AFTER RADIATION

There's a sunset worth watching down the street—
we could put on our shoes and go see. Or climb barefoot
through the bedroom window, for a better look.

Then we can lie down, heads up,
elbows propped on the west pitch of the roof
in clear view of the neighbours.

We'll share a beer while tilting side to side,
our bum cheeks burning on the still-hot asphalt,
our pale skin splotching under thin summer shorts.

My friend Shannon said beer
was the one thing her mum liked to drink
during treatment.

So I tried it. Beer, proof that God loves us
and wants us to be happy.
But it still hurt going down.

Tonight, let's have that Belgian framboise,
the lambic one we drank young, in Montreal,
with the raspberries brewed right in.

Let's savour both sour and sweet
the pink-gold alloy bubbling
down our grateful throats.

But Belgium's in trouble:
Man-bombs are blowing up airports and stations,
impenitent killers hide in plain sight.

Here on the roof, we'll toast our salvation.
Backlit by beauty,
as hope lustrates the sky.

I LOVE YOU, DR. THEODORAKIS

When we met, I wasn't doing well.
Four weeks in, or was it five, of daily radiation.
My body a gaunt shell.

I was the pale shadow in that shabby consult room
beside my vibrant friend
with her new haircut.

Then you came in, bringing a Greek island:
blue skies and pelicans, black cats and
whitewashed houses. Old ladies beckoning

Swim! Swim! by the turquoise sea,
my dad telling his pelican belly-can joke
so long ago, when I was young and invincible.

You laughed and you hugged me. Said I was *So strong!*
Told me the ward upstairs was full of weak men
who couldn't handle as much as me.

I think the tide turned that day.
The air felt warmer when we walked outside.
I heard a seagull. It didn't hurt to breathe.

BED

We wait for snow and it doesn't come.
All of December it rains.

Toronto, fat city near a filthy lake, has never been taller,
more bouncing with people, condos, and wonderfully foreign dirty movies.

Streetcar by our window. The glass rattles twice.
We go back to white sheets still warm, stay there all afternoon.

Listen to truck and children noises, smell rotten bok choy,
ten-for-a-dollar Chinatown oranges. We move closer.

Two years. Tops. The oncologist said.
We stared at the negative: two blocks of shadow on a sheet of snow.

EARLY EVENING

Things slow down for us. Television, nod-reading,
sleeping, not much need for food. In bed next to you,
I reach through the dark, feel for the heat of your ribs.

I know of course that you are dying.
Figure if I wake you from your morphine slumber
you may stay longer. If I hold the kiss, inhale

as if you are my last kiss and breath, your lips
will stay soft, face less skeletal.

We'll have breakfast by candlelight,
the sun rising instead.

WELCOME BACK TO CANCERLAND
—after Rabbis Phyllis and Michael Sommer

The word *oncologist* made my heart fall through my knees.
The word *relapse* is like the word *collapse.*

The definition of *good* is a Talmudic one.
Believe that prayer is prayer.

The routines are the same.
Things you wanted not to remember.

Up here on 5E, you live moment by moment.
Amazed at how fast and slow it all seems to go.

It feels like last time, like the times before.
But it's not.

Dear cells, please proceed with your healing.
You can never beg too many blessings.

ENVY

She is green
because those cells are so far
from her that she can
dream about flowers and frozen lasagnas
and gift cards for pretty nails.

So she does not hold
my hand or smile
knowingly, but instead

talks about the dress that fits
perfectly, the vacation that starts the same
day as my fifth treatment and the long life
she plans

OFFERING
for my mother

I wonder what you know of that thousandth burnt offering:
the canoe people it talks as if, had Atlantis never drowned

your own fig tree could be counted in its echo. This living mecca
of a Solomon'd people I can do nothing to save, you mind this

burnt Jerusalem still weary in your dreams, far from what would give
long life, to an animal that won't hold the melancholy of things

nobody has made, or has made into the horse-drawn disorder in your belly,
It's raw, sorry, the doctor says, *i think this won't be good news*

You had no chance to leave codes in paintings, no chance in seven decades
to yield the sweetest name back to sorcery, like Bowie's transients,

how they mime from my mirrored head, the legend of your leaving
and of course, it is silly to mourn you, still alive,

with that thousandth burnt of the twelve thousandth offering leaving me
transcribed to the healed. I will give you what you have not asked,

except by the accidental click of your tongue to the roof of your brave
mouth as you yawn this post-surgical hunger of three weeks of pain.

You knew to be brave, you knew who knew your bravery. I will give you
what you have not asked. See how I slip you into my breast pocket,

the great anchor of a crime for which those doctors won't pay.
See how you crumple like a picture of these two Plutos proper: pre & post pure

planet at the synth moving me to pity, this last faith, my prescription printed
from some internet café. I've broken again what you believe unbreakable

and now I am not counted among the Solomon'd people
who leave you to enter that faithless theatre alone.

I have abandoned what you now remind me
was always meant to unfurl like smoke, all the unreasonable phrases

I hide from you. I wish this anomaly in your belly into sad-mad emojis
I throw it aside with the good things of unreadable ends.

Just for today, I'd like to be more caring of humans than flowers.
I long for a room far away from the reception desk.

Where are the years and the work of your hands
now? What could seal shut the fabled outcome?

I raise you to ride the shoulders of a sacred need that I cannot fathom
out of trapezing angels, out of that cloud-hung perpetuity in praise of sorrow,

in these earth-stained, invisible helpers to whom you'd owe all of what survives.
I raise you to ride toward a direct challenge of these red lights.

Tell me you'll do it all. Dear outline of womb, dear mouth to speak me whole.
Dear heart-song, dear exit to follow home. I know already, we are blood.

The black-cloaked guards that walk past your room supplant that future
of poplar stencils giving you wings. These songs we sing

at your bedside today, things hungered for, things no one has made
but which we all share, now loosed in our bones

insisting you grab hold of the upper-hand bars. So you're new strength,
so you're yet another all-morning rebirth of things the surgeon ignored.

Straight-spined someday, I'll speak the legend or some other foolish thing,
speak your last imago, or the waking harmonica the fig trees still remember.

Your cure comes yet you are not the same. Your cure has replaced you.
And here you are: alive, a thousandth burnt offering, a thousand octaves faded.

NUMBERS LESS THAN ZERO

My father has said few things I remember. Our laughter emptied into some stormed volt, my head: a menagerie for every Icarus returned bearing the gift of empty hands and repentance. I imagine the cocking noise of scalpels falling into metal cans. Thing is asking for miracles when the miracle feels like theft. The man never gave what the man never gave and never mind the logic, the circles it must make. I'll make of logic whatever. I'll make of logic the sky and its mute thunder. I'll make the days as my father made the garden. The gardener tending the vast spaces from headstone to headstone, ringing the Sunday bell. My father was cloud, was rain, swapping places with the street parking, encircling the dunes. I remember things but not what my father said. He said two years. He said cancer. The way death makes sense of nothing, not even the scattered planes. I remember nothing my father has said. He's spoken and I don't know when to call the priests for their token of last rites. Unless you want them, Mama. I know what you've been that is better, Mama. How you were drawn from the farrow by men in vests begging your bones return the DDT to its caloric laboratory. I remember the story of us, living where the storm lays down its fret, the former lives of shadows dragging our names through us, our unmake intoning at the bazaar. I think of nothing my father has said. Think of us: evergreens, shaking our things, raising drink, raising some ringed *amen!* from the dead.

WHAT DO FRIDA KAHLO AND MY MOTHER HAVE IN COMMON?
"I hope the exit is joyful and I hope never to return."—Frida Kahlo

Where do all the breasts go? Found to be cancerous, excised from women's bodies, for a time they lie on a tin tray. A mound of flesh, a nipple, skin...my mother's skin—pink lying in a lump, in her own blood. Do all the breasts go in one big biohazard bag, piled on top of the other? Frightened! They have never been on their own, call out to their sister but she cannot hear them over all that weeping.

What of legs and arms? Gangrene set in. Blackened. Even so they are missed. Phantom limbs still itch. Hands reach out with nothing left to scratch. The one that remains mourns its companion.

It is not supposed to be like this. We were to go together. All of us at once, not one body part at a time. Yet the remaining bits must carry on, wear bras made for two breasts, pants for two legs and sweaters for two arms.

Once a part of us has left it matters not—for our focus is on the living. There will be no one there to grieve as a man in overalls and gloves incinerates our loved ones. No prayers said, flowers offered, ashes scattered. Does this mean that we have one foot in the grave? One breast in the grave? For even if no one says it, we all know that if not caught soon enough a new word will be introduced.

DEAR NEPHEW

a raven flew into your birdcage chest
and having grown silently large
it pressed against

esophagus   crushing

      vocal chords

insistent it pushed
your heart   unrelenting
in the crowding of a lung
that no one can find

my sweet boy you are death's companion
first your father and his lungs
and now you

I think of all the years you meant to live
the way you held us in hope and said that
you were 100% committed to staying
but I knew it would take more than we had
that your body would become the scene of a crime
where we would find ourselves

unwilling
witnesses
with paperwork
on our fridge

DO NOT RESUSCITATE

in bold letters

we became accomplices in a reality
that said there was no one to call
one where the sunflowers have the face
of your friend and a woman sits reading
the newspaper while wearing purple

coat   a leopard tam
you said that she never speaks
her interruptions heard as pages turning
even so   it was hard for you to follow TV shows
you wanted a storyboard
a map of the merging so you could follow along

in this liminal space we share   I sit
in a chair beside you   thinking I should get up
sort that bookcase but tired from trail of care I pass thought to you
and you say you see me

in the corner
and when I ask
what am I doing
you say looking
at the bookcase

you said that I am always looking
at the bookcase   perhaps I was hoping

        for another ending

but now even the unfinished
box of Raisin Bran
leads me back to you
your bread-crumb trail of things
cellphones   laptops
artwork   lamps
what to do with wallets
their contents worn
all things we must now find
something to do with
when what we really want is you

        we are left

with questions   so ask

did we do enough

the response is always the same
I hear the raven flutter his wings
he has you now and he wants you to fly

THE CLOUDS REFUSE TO BREAK

In the dead
of night, on the floor
of that hospital wing,

the only audible thing,
not the living, not their breathing, too slight
under the monitors' beeping.

Our mother's belly, a balloon
rising skyward, growing larger
as it rose.

We needed a translator
for terms one hopes
never to utter.

How to say *omentum,*
incision, epithelial, ascites, ex-
cision? The translator arrived,

delivered the same words—
paracentesis, peritoneum—
in a different language, failing

to elucidate a single thing.
Never has a silent room
echoed so loudly.

In the morning, across the river,
three smokestacks coughing back
to life.

One side of her abdomen
tucked against the other, stapled
like a poster to a phone pole.

One bird changes direction
and all
head south, the way

one word
changes the tenor
of all that follow.

NIL BY NONE

She is in a place, she thinks. Where? An inappropriate
term. Other questions fail her. She feels like she's...no,
wrong again, she begins once more. Elemental
whiteness. Theoretical whiteness, utter absence of
darkness in which contrast has been abandoned; she
does not know that she can see. Confined to an
infinitesimal space in which she cannot stretch or turn,
though she is not uncomfortable. She is limbless, no
remainder, but gropes beyond herself in blind phantom
extension. Pellucid. She is unbound by an extraordinary
deliverance from feeling. She is standing, she lies prone,
she breathes, she is drowning, she rushes toward, she
waits until, she is dressed for a date, she has no skin or
bone, she is floating, she is rooted, buried, she thinks of
herself, she is no longer of, iconic, but as if, unbonding
the way electrons slip from an unstable atom—if
nothing can be said to explode against a singular
expanse of emptiness discernibly. An idea. Nil by naught.

How long? Duration is immeasurably slow or, once
and for all, instantaneous. Had she been flailing at
something before this became and movement ceased, or
movement grew imperceptibly rapid, unrecordable? She
is certain there was prior experience by which she
defined quantities, but the belief is disappointing.
Reference has evaporated. She is unsure of was and will
be. She is not here, she convinces herself that she is
thinking this right now. She is not here. Infinite sphere,
centre everywhere without circumference.

GRAVELLY BAY

The ferryman flags your car
into line, signals
to shut off
your engine,
shift
into wait.

You slump
into the steering wheel, stare
at the landscape rolling out
its postcard images
that as you look
seem to fly
into place

or is it you, not flying
but silting?

Sand, bits of shell.

    ***

Step out of the
car, close
the door
        click
is that salt on the air?

The dog died in his basket
beside the kiln in your studio.

But what you remember
is the day before;
the beagle planting himself
at the woodshed beside the bucket
of rotting gingko seed.

Gravelly Bay is like that.
A stopping place. The one
before-the-last. The anteroom.

Or (and this seems more likely)
a gesture, a continuity—
to ward off the panic you still replay:
begging the nurse
to up your father's morphine
that time before the last.

You lean into the car's hood, still warm.

    ***

Behind you cars shudder then stop.
A tense shifting: the past
with its rust,
its bald tires, chrome
and overheated
engines
lines up
at the terminal.

You know the drill. Car
by car the ferryman signals
travellers on board. Bets
are on the blue Toyota
getting waved ahead.

Who will make it?
Who'll be left behind?

    ***

The skin around your eyes
grew thin

the year you worked
on the portrait of your father.

The way he leaned
into his image made it clear
how long he'd carried his abandonment: all

his life. Birds and animals have their own equations.
The beagle chose his particulars—
flopping down beside the smelly gingko.

Early November. Gift-warm. You'd been cycling.

Then it was winter. And again
the neighbour's black cat who doesn't mind
weather. Very black on very cold.
And again crow's outline against the sky.

Even the dark has a boundary.

    ***

Somebody's golden retriever
breaks from the lineup, bounds
onto the bay's rocky outcrop,
to the edge—
the drop-off.

Dog in silhouette, rind of lemon
light, nose pointed up, away—

The moon cuts free. The dark
sets out in its boat: crow
rides the current.

AN ODE AN ELEGY A CANCER

tendering my burden

be it down on flesh taken in the lens and made a permanence that makes the
       eye cry out
at the end

lead wafers in the round machine much the same as stitching and its eye an
       aperture
in the lead

machine in skirts of curtains ones from heights where opera can be seen by
       faces of half
faces these are the same as the opening where light that has no light comes
       through

trees of my abdomen redness of lasers mark the cross thrown down the holy
       water
that burns invisible

and scars? There are no scars only what is left when forest is taken away

skin of my belly in my hands lifts away from itself as I stand with pants to
       knees and with
my underpants down from my dugs and me in my eyes in my mirror

this is the age in the middle when I no longer fear my image in its sunset the
       sloughing
of years goes unnoticed brown bits of flesh take my face and my eyes upon my
       eyes are
a Mona Lisa

shall I stroll the rolling stones of Ross Bay that in morning can be heard one on
       one
another on another   ones the D-9 cats spread to keep the hungry ocean from
       taking land
unto itself

sea is no gristling red woman whose glory bleeds upon the water and in its
            smallest sound
is each round vessel opening through the door of water from farness to the eye

I have left behind my x-rays in their albums that in their own dust resign themselves
to the yellow pale of eggs

the way the body's clothes when taken will hold a little warm

the bruised gun of evening nothing more

ROCKBOUND
for Pat

We sit in my flower garden   surrounded by dew
soaked blossoms.   Misted sunlight streaks   long
shafts of silver mirrored   throughout your hair.
This is the morning   you tell me that you will start
chemotherapy   wanting   acknowledgement
aside from the doctor who sat quietly   knowing
the silent growth.   I give you   those words
slip off my tongue   like river rocks   the ones
I collect with you on our many walks.   Words drop
though the air   splash into blood   comfort you
like the red fleece blanket   wrapped around
your shoulders. The red startling against your frame's
thin mantle   skin hung across protruding bones
like a loose-fitting sheet.   We comment on a slug
edging its way across the concrete path   a distraction
from this sharp place.   Antennae jut forward sensing
its way.   I think how easily I could squish its body
stop   this slow slime trail   body so sleek
no bones   to protect it from the   smash of a rock
but that would offend you.   Such a death   so small
so unnecessary.   My heart grips   for words
while poppies   drip petals   at your feet.

GATECRASHER

Maybe only one invader slipped through
masked in mucky feed, or a horse trailer
stowaway from god-knows-where.

Its burred offspring thrives in dirt
sapped by the scrape and whack
of former tenants who carved

their names in concrete, staked
kennels on spent soil, milled cash
from dog flesh—mounds of thirsty pups

in a skinny hot pen. The weed's alien
absent from guides: local
and far afield. Unchecked

it's a mass of flower fireworks: radiant
Catherine wheels and blue burst
from this flourish

that parches earth with its guzzle,
leaves native fescue sere and shoved aside
as it drapes over pales

to annex our pasture. I rip armfuls
of garlands; loosed seeds shower
like sequins. I sow as I pluck and spade.

Even sleep is specked with unblinking
blue eyes: dream runners
slim-legged and spurred

with stars that prick gloves, socks,
and stud the dog's wool.
We become carriers

like the scalpel a friend suspected
had pearled healthy tissue, quickened
the spread, told me this

without bitterness or blame
just wanted, she said, for wisdom
to understand—

Yet there's no reading of it, no
cunning, just growth so fecund
all around it withers.

But I'll take her unclaimed anger
to augment my own.

FLESH AND FLUIDS

After forty minutes
in the magnetron
I wait for the world

to quieten around me,
for someone to offer
access to the miraculous.

Are there coffins
in the crypt? How long
does dying take?

I still intend
to climb the rock fall—
no one can take my place.

This cancer is like
a loved one held hostage
and never allowed to go.

MASTECTOMY

Fortunate one, you were chosen victim of
the worst injustice: life hates life. Your breasts
took suddenly that hue called pit,
the opposite colour of human flesh.
Your life was forcing on you freedom
from your life: and yet
it was for freedom that fire
became man, said the sad sage
with his never consummated burning.
Looking at you, I was given understanding
that my prayers for you were for another,
for a kind injustice, for myself: Give me,
the prayers were saying, always
a way to work, meaning: Part the crowd.
Part me the crowd in the terminal ward,
in the academy part it, make way for me
and at the trough give me my part,
the part that is the whole, make me
the pillar of fire, the column of water
that walks the land
undrunk, crystalline and revolving, free.
Make me
the one who has the world in hand
as the hourglass has the disease of sand.
Make her, make us, but make me
the container that cannot exist,
the vessel to hold all things shapely and forever
let me walk here and see.

THE VOICE OF THE FOX

Each year when the grey sky lets loose
its first snow, I listen for his voice.

That winter the old farm lent me its solitude.
We were depleted—isolated.

Each day I walked the barren fields
between rows of pine.

Their heavy scent made my head throb
as if it had replaced my heart.

I welcomed the indifference of the snow.
I was insulated: no hospitals,

no scalpels, no poison
to kill what was killing me.

Then he appeared—a blaze of orange
floating over the drifting land.

Velvet-black muzzle piercing forward.
White-tail-tip brushing the cold air like a wand.

He angled his head to one side—caught me
in the circumference of his amber eye.

His voice—a silent implosion,
filled me with his rapture—life without fear.

CLOG: A SERIES

He is the skeleton in your cloakroom,
Clog, the black sheep in your family,
the one your aunts never bring up
over coffee and lemon slice,

I wonder what he's up to now,

where's he livin'
these days?

He is lost on their tongues,
and from their minds, but he is there:
a photo crammed
between calendars and wrapping paper,
his sticky fingerprints
stained on the pages
of your favourite book.

If you close your eyes
and breathe,
you can smell him.

        *

He is horny, Clog,
and he is his own
master, getting himself
up during dry spells,
hot breath beer
grunts calluses on soft
flesh, hard staring at
the bath mat

that   needs   a

wash

                    ohgod needs
ah

Clog sows his oats too
and plenty of them,
gives new meaning
to the word dead/

beat

the patter of a

thousand perfect shadows
in his wake.

    *

Rough
and tumble, and
angry   drifting
Clog along twisted
city streets
and arteries,
blown into
town, stumbling

drunk, and stinking
through his pores,
drooling through
his tongue,
eyes like
marbles hitting
the sun, his hands
hitting everything
they can.

It's all he knows,

he knows.

    *

Not quite sweet as
sugar, BoneDaddy
coaxing them
one by one to
take him in
to put him up.

He would give them
the world (just
wouldn't say which)
while oysters drunk
and swollen slide
down throats at earls:

if you touch me

i will
           make
     you
        dance

By morning, his
search is on again,
an empty bed
the only clue,
they're bags of bones
in the corner,
Clog's stench tattooed
in their pores.

WORDS WE DON'T SAY

I

The men in our family
don't say *I love you.*

So when your aunt called,
explained your diagnosis,
informed me that you refused
treatment,

I didn't call.

I had no words to share.

I'm bad with goodbyes,
and we don't say
I love you.

I spent the next week,
trying to craft a conversation;
attempting to invent dialogue
that we would never have.

Hours before I would get the news,
you appeared in my dream.

Skinny you,
urging me to persevere.

You didn't see the irony in the situation.

I pointed out that
"I'm the one who
was supposed to die young,
not you.

I'll see you soon—"
Awakening to answer a phone

call meant to inform me of what
you had just told me.

When your dad got sick,
as doctors were confused,
I assumed it was a case of
"Like father, like son."

Your aunt passed me the phone.
I could almost hear him leaving this earth
through the receiver.

We told one another jokes—
that's what men in this family do.
Competing to see who was best
at pretending to be strong.

His sister thought it was a scare,
but we understood—this was it.
Handing the phone back to your aunt,
I told him what I told you,

"I'll see you soon."

The men in our family
don't say *I love you*.

II

We met our mother's mother through photographs.
She looked like a prettier version of her daughters.
Death gave her permission to be perfect,
our interactions with her were edited nostalgia.

Her husband said little of her.
When we asked who she was,
he made us fetch photo albums—

even after his first stroke took his sight.

She was a teacher, mother, hardworking, God-fearing person who died because Third World hospitals didn't have facilities to properly treat breast cancer back then.

When I realized that he witnessed his wife go that way, eight-year-old me stopped asking questions.

III

My father was once diagnosed with cancer. The day before he was to have surgery, before beginning radiation treatments, my mom, a bunch of her friends prayed over him. After his surgery, doctors said that his cancer disappeared. True story. That's some bullshit. Seriously. Motherfucker must have superpowers.

THAT DAY MY MAMA LOST HER MIND

Accused us all of robbing her
of what? Things? Money? Dignity?
For placing her in what she swears
was a *locked ward* and saying we
were in *cahoots* with doctors, nurses
the daughter of her silenced roommate-
so-suddenly-gone-*palliative*.

Why! she wanted to know
demanding, *How could you?*
All day long. *That's what I get?*

Still she let me uncork sweet
purple varnish remover to swab
toenails and disappear the rusty pink
of southern Florida then clip and file
right down to baby nail
trying to relieve those impacted
then slather her swollen feet with cream.

CHAISE

"My chaise..." (she says)
...has buttons of green silk..."
                    it is careless—how we
bear riches
"Look..."
                    pillows of velvet,
                    cushioned, soft, a casement full
                    of ferns and sun—

—And a green glass bowl on the table?—(I say)

"Green crystal...full...of apricots...pears..."

—And a pedestal phone, like those forties films. Ivory and gold, and it rings—

"all day!"
—all day!—(we say)

—with lovers and friends!—

"While I...lounge around..."

—on your velvet chaise—

"...all day..."

—dressed in—?

"...silk, and gauze..."

—You wear earrings of jade, to match the chaise—

"...and a...gold
                    ...en...chain...to...
                                        catch...the...

        ssu- u-...

       ...sssu- u-..."
—Nurse! *Nurse!*—

          needle—

        and

                   she

            drifts

            it is
                ferny, filled
                   it is

                                 golden

              in the room
           where the green
        chaise
         lounges
                on a silky
      rug on its own

glossy page in the Sears
catalogue. It is
twelve
hundred dollars. It is not
her bed
in the palliative ward.
            buttons of green silk—
Is not
the fern that litters the sill.
            apricots, pears—
Not the machine
that beeps all day.
            with voices of friends—
It is not the
cough
            cushioned, soft—

that will not
leave
though the sun pours its gold
into this hospital
room, across
her bed
for free.

            all day
            all day

A DAUGHTER'S LULLABY

Hushaby, my little one
Hushaby, my darling
Hushaby,
Hushaby,
Hushaby, my little...
—Origin unknown

We end as we began
together in a hospital bed
this labour of breaths
an air of patience.
We fit on this single bed. The length of me
along the length of you. As before,
framed by the safety of aluminum rails on both sides
barriers that contain us.

Nearly forty years ago to this July day
you pushed me from your womb, a labour
in the dawn of a hospital room;
Montreal's humid traffic pressed the streets.
The nurse gave you opiates then,
a propulsion of relief
from the invisible angular tip of a syringe.
Again, the nurses supply you with opiates.
Dilaudid flows into your bloodstream
accessed by a small patch in the shape of a butterfly
landed as a pinprick near your collarbone.

I remember once kissing the length of your arm
from wrist to shoulder, my child's mouth
landing like a swallowtail following a mineral lick.
My passion made you blush.

In this bed, my left arm curves an archway
framing the crown of your head. My right arm
drapes across a looseness where your breast once was.
We have lain in variations of this formation
before. Nights when I was sick, a flu, convulsions

no surprise to find you not sleeping
a vigilant mother on the bedroom floor till morning.

Your breath, when I catch it,
is the malty stench of tinned meal replacements
and has cured me of any desire for vanilla, strawberry or chocolate,
also the flavours of ice cream in cup-sized portions
in the communal fridge in the *Family Room*,
a place to convene for coffee, tea, sweets,
a break from the disciplined orientation of hospital rooms:
beds lined perpendicular to walls, nightstand to the left:
the potted plants, greeting cards, photo albums,
cheery balloons tied to plastic sticks.
Nightstand to the right: a pyramid of Ensure cans.

Two nights in a row I've slept
in the reclined cushion of a La-Z-Boy chair.
The nurse brought me a blanket
when I wished for opium.

I've eaten starchy snacks from clear plastic containers
bought at the gift shop, and watched *Late Night*
with him or him or him on a small white TV
suspended from an articulated arm above your bed.
The comedians made me laugh.

Suffocation—the thought of taking an action
to end this—flitters in the room. A momentary impulse
I recall once combined with teenage rage,
something about
wanting to smash your head into a wall.

We share your room with no one.
The blankets and sheets on the other beds
tucked neatly as "hospital corners,"
you learned that much from nursing training.

It seems excessive, all this open space,
the limitless ice cream, the tranquility,
the opiates, and the gentle hospice light.
The last few hours spent
side by side
beginning as we end.

THE LANGUAGE OF SPARROWS

Your sister was claimed by cancer.

We plant seedlings
by her grave in April,
when Spring seduces
with all its promise,
moisten the ground
with a jug of water
and say how, years from now,
a bush will burst and flower,
be home to a family of sparrows,
each knowing the other by name.

I ask you if birds have names,
like *Alice, Brent, Jessica* and *James,*
if mother and father bird
call them in when it rains,
say *settle here in branches*
amid the leaves that keep you dry—
not in English, mind you,
or any other human tongue
but in the language of sparrows;
each trill, each warbling,
a repartee,
a crafted conversation of the minds.

EMPTYING THE DRAINS

The receptacles hang from her sides,
odd ornaments or

bulbs from a baster, attached
by elastic tubes

that siphon lymph and blood
from wounds

that used to be her breasts.
Careful now.

She can't raise her arms so it's tough
to do alone though

some women must. *Careful.* Pinch
near her rib

and draw down
to milk the liquid,

thick red from the first days
now washing

out closer to clear. A warm iron
smell still rich

in the bathroom. Sneak a peak
at the yanked

scar on her *careful* sharp wince
if the tug

is too severe. 4 ml is down
from yesterday

and good, no sign of infection. Measure
then rinse

the egg vessels, gently settle
the baubles back

into place at her sides. We will never speak
of the intimacies

of these weeks, she won't meet
my eye while

I ease the nightshirt back over
her bowed head.

I ABANDON MY WIFE IN THE HOSPITAL

I follow the steps I see in front of me
They are deep and well-defined
They show an undefined but straight path
What has gone through me will never return.
—Sepultura, "Primitive Fugitive"

Since the diagnosis, I've had so many
Arguments without her that I consider
The wall to be my peer, a mirror slightly
Less distorted than the bottom of a Żywiec
Bottle to view the future better than
A Magic 8-Ball's predilection to foresee
A lifetime's hatred of life is rewarded
With a lifetime of being alone. When my mind
Boils outside of the chemo ward and I flee
I follow the steps I see in front of me

Etched in icy sidewalks directly
To the bar, excuse already waiting.
Since the diagnosis, I've been assured
Many times by nurses and friends
(Doctors know better) that it's just
As hard on spouses confined
By the disease because they are also
Helpless in the face of uncertainty.
I'm aware they are trying to be kind;
They are deep and well-defined

With the best of intentions, compassion
Even. "Spouses shouldn't suffer in silence,"
They said to me without irony or disdain.
Yet when it comes, we shiver. I stop
Answering messages as I'm immobile
In the face of sympathy, aftermath
Of compassionate looks that burn. Since
Her diagnosis, I can't even see the cover
Of the *The Cancer Ward* without spitting wrath.
They show an undefined but straight path

To hope when in faith, they praise helplessness.
If I, fickle, were truly without agency then
I couldn't run away. Doctors know better
But idiots know more. *Sarcoma* and *results*
Are the most important words since her diagnosis.
Sickness is a process and my fury will discern
This puzzle. I cling to the belief that it can be solved,
Petty horrors redeemed, life and death variegate
In a barren apartment and hate to learn
What has gone through me will never return.

HOUSEGUEST

the baby won't sleep
& my longtime companion
the cat
has expired
by the end, his body'd
become so bony, so light
that when I lifted him
to my chest
it was as if he'd already
taken flight   *birdlike*

what's left of my old friend
is buried, somewhere,
in a heap of laundry
that's invaded
our basement
where the dripping pipes
disrupt the damp quiet
where the sow bugs
curl up in their suits
of grey armour
where i stand
sometimes for hours
my hands over my face

is this your life?
this can't be your life.

we could continue
this tour
of the house, except
my husband's resting
on the couch
& some of you
might be squeamish
or surprised
you might not

recognize
him
so let's not
poke our noses in
to say *hi, hello,*
what the hell happened to you?

it's day 29
in Treatment Time,
his throat's so ravaged
by radiation
he feeds
through a tube
an appendage
that hangs
above his belly button
held in place by a gadget
best described as a balloon

a landfill has erupted
in our house & i half-expect
a bear
to claw its way up
the stairs

oh, as much as I
would like for you
to stay, as much as I
want you to stay,
as much as I
would like to cling
to you all night,
please, please,
come again
another day
when that volt
of vultures
has pushed on

when the bear
has gone back
to its den, when,
when,
we can dream again.

THERE'LL BE NO KNOCK ON THE DOOR

You would have loved this mint-and-cauliflower taco
You would have loved this owl cup, this espresso
We are in a small city, we park everywhere for free,
we can lock up, lucky, and just go.

I biked by our old apartment and remembered
how much my cat hated your cat, and how much
your cat didn't care. I remember we jogged around
Christie Pits when we had sad days.

I wanted to call you the night of the final Hip show.
You were still alive then and I can't
Believe I didn't call. I sat between my aging parents,
who didn't know the band, and a five-year-old

who was bored. I was without courage. I was
trying to get through the stress of living
this amazing life full of love, I remember
crying during "Grace, Too" when Gord cried

seeing the fear of death in his face.
I saw your mom today. She said that
when Leonard Cohen died you said
I hope we're on the same train.

Right before you died, you said I want
some water. And they gave you a glass.
And you said, *No, I want the good stuff*
So they gave you bottled water.

And you said, *No, the good stuff.*
And they said, *What do you mean?*
and you said, *I want peace.*

THE SUMMER GUYS

It's the only way I can think of them
our small early-morning gathering
in the dead middle of dark winter
looking for the first light in the sky
sun a fly ball you can't see to catch.

Four of us sitting inside the alcove
just outside our Radiation Suite 22
waiting with full bladders, wanting
to get up and dance rather than settle
into idle chatter of how-is-it-going?

Could be a quartet of bleary retirees
huddled for coffee at the local mall.
Could be a group for a poker game
and considering it's prostate cancer
poker is really not far off the mark.

Yep, these four verses are really for
the summer guys who laughed me
through my 33 treatments at old 22.
Bill, Richard, jovial George and Ed.
Happy a new day happened to them.

LOOK BOTH WAYS

Sometimes, navigating through all the ways
they hurry in to fix us—the cuts, the burns
the radical prostatectomy surgery and radiation
the needles, the pills, the pilots and the PSAs

I sometimes close my eyes and dream a time
when medicine has moved far from where it
is stuck now, when someone has what I have
but gets treated in a way I wouldn't recognize

and I ask myself if that patient will ever pause
to look back (as I have paused to look ahead)
to maybe feel sad at the way we were treated
or amazed at how we sang in such a darkness.

MASTECTOMY

Half a year later,
Meg says, this time
the joke's on whoever stole her bikini
from the Turkish bath in Bursa.
What the hell will they do
with an extra boob?

LETTERS TO THE INSURANCE ADJUSTER

Oct. 21

Dear Insurance Adjuster:

Thank you for getting in touch with me via voice mail. I'm not a little alarmed to note that you sound approximately twelve years old. Far be it for me to be accused of ageism, but my disability is of some consequence, so could my case file be allocated to a grown-up?

Sincerely yours,

Case File 717185

Oct. 22

Dear Insurance Adjuster:

Thank you for letting me know that my disability claim has been accepted until Oct. 24th. I will do my best to fit the estimated six weeks of recovery time into two days.

Sincerely yours,

Case File 717185

Oct. 25

Dear Insurance Adjuster:

Thank you for form #73 that you request I fax you. I understand that you are delighted by the seeming ease of the tick-box system.

Perhaps the pen really is mightier than the sword. Death by bean-counting?

I have duly placed ticks in the corresponding boxes for "patient can incline head at a 45 degree angle" and "patient is capable of manipulating two or more fingers on one or more hands."

How this translates into "patient is her usual lively, curious, energetic self, ready to leap around the classroom and to write pages of comments on student essays, during repeated twelve-hour workdays," I am not exactly sure. Perhaps form #74 will provide an answer to this perplexity.

Sincerely yours,

Case File 717185

P.S. Having no fax machine in my bedroom, where I am presently marooned, I will seal form #73 into a snail-mail envelope and have my husband post it. My present ambulatory skills disallow the two blocks to the mailbox.

Oct. 30

Dear Insurance Adjuster:

Thank you for your visit earlier today, and for tracking mud onto my clean floors. No invitation had been extended, but you do have certain rights, I understand. You seemed exuberant to see a freshly polished dining table and seasonal decorations.

I dust a room a day for exercise. My husband keeps the carpet clean because I frequently nap on it.

The decorations will remain up through the next months, as I haven't the energy to put them away. In any case, the witches and bats, dark souls, seem fitting. My imaginative vision see/k/s death, not birth. Death to germs, death to unsanitary conditions. The filth on your muddy boots.

Because I am well enough to clean does not mean that I am well enough to work unless you can obtain for me part-part-part-part-part-time custodial services at the university.

Sincerely yours,

Case File 717185

Nov. 5

Dear Insurance Adjuster:

No, yes, I am without diagnosis still. It might be lymphoma. It might not. Like plucking petals from a daisy to see if he loves me.

Thank you for checking up on me. It's nice to feel needed. I hope you will recommend my fashion plate to all other clients under your care: dirty sweats, unwashed hair, and an ice pack wrapped in a tea towel on the head. You understand that, as much as I would have liked to invite you in for tea, I simply could not.

Sincerely yours,

Case File 717185

Nov. 8

Dear Insurance Adjuster:

Thank you for pointing out the egregiousness of my doctor's claim that I am sick. Sotto voce, you note that some doctors are more than generous, allowing five years for cancer, two months for, say, a cold. I appreciate your desire to have a rapport with me, I hope you won't mind if I suggest that you should go to bed early, eat all your greens, and listen to your elders, including wise doctors.

Sincerely yours,

Case File 717185

Nov. 10

Dear Insurance Adjuster:

Thank you for advising me that further disability payments will cease without corresponding paperwork from my doctor. What, pray, do you wish, as my file folder must be a foot high with scans, biopsies, treatments tried? My doctor is as sick of this as I am.

Perhaps a Xerox of the planetary outcropping on my infected leg, should I be able to drape it over the Xerox machine? A note from me suggesting that my doctor is not sick, though she is despairing, weary, frankly stumped? A poem about return to health being less than linear?

Sincerely yours,

Case File 717185

Nov. 14

Dear Insurance Adjuster:

Thank you for suggesting that an immediate return to work will speed my recovery. I am too weary to fight you.

I will plan mini-lectures of not more than five minutes to allow for nausea and diarrhea. As my classes are of four hours' duration and I've not been awake for more than three hours in a row, I'll do my best to find pertinent YouTube clips to show during the last hour. Any suggestions?

Perhaps, given the stresses of university life, students will enjoy napping along with me, dreaming of a parallel universe in which evil is vanquished, and Health reigns supreme.

Sincerely yours,

Case File 717185

Dec. 1

Dear Insurance Adjuster:

Thank you for wondering what I am doing at a health spa while you play Mr. Scrooge cutting me thinner and thinner disability cheques.

Trust me that this is therapy, not pleasure. Trust me that this place is as much a workhouse as yours. Trust me that I am struggling to get better, to hasten my recovery, so that your cheques can thin to nothingness, just as you would wish during this festive time, when all good little boys get what they ask for.

Sincerely yours,

Case File 717185

P.S. Please find a new pair of fingerless gloves, size extra small, under separate cover. The best of the season to you and yours.

CANCER WARD WAITING ROOM

Groundhogs in rows
Some with stocking caps
To hide
Chemical pattern baldness

Cheekbones cut glass
Cutting weight
Regretting every diet wish
And calorie count

Japanese snow
Lay dusting and denying
First spring shoots
Imposing a turn
Of the cycle

A hole for each
Making a tunnel
With the sun at one end

Each pokes up its head
And hopes desperately
To see its shadow

DAY 1,096

Today is the first day of the rest of your life.
Today is your chance to make the world a better place.
Today is the dawning of a new age.
Today is a new day.
Today is Day One.

Today is a red X on a calendar
Marking the days
Like an inevitability, hopefully.
Afraid to stop marking before reaching the end.

Today is one day removed from the oncologist with the quiet voice
And one day closer to being able to say
Cancer-free
And mean it.
If I can convince myself to mean it.

Today is like any other day in the life of uncertainty.
Today is a reminder of the psychologist saying,
"You aren't depressed; your life is just terrible."

Today is MY life, no matter how terrible.
My life. My day. My calendar, X by X.
Each a kiss of life, and empathy, and survivor's guilt.

Today is a dropped ball, 7-2-5, never stop playing double play.
Because never stop playing.

Three years is a long time to wait
But today is another day where that wait wasn't curtailed,
Short-circuited, and interrupted.

Today is one day safer.
Today is one day freer.
Today is one day closer
To day 1,096,

Also known as

Day One.

A VIRUS FROM OUTER SPACE

Language
is a virus
from outer space.

Language
is a pursuer
of covert aims.

Language
frames our
virus as poetic.

Language
tapers our
vicious frames.

Language
for a sum is
a corrupt sieve.

Language
for us promises
a curative.

HEALTH STORM

My husband's 9th melanoma recurrence?
Climate change hits the Wizard of Oz.

We can't transform until we close the door.
Just as we tug it open to the torrent
comes the whiff of petrichor,
then the shock of rain, wind, and ice needles
as we slam it behind us. Our wills seem to precipitate
as we, like children in a house lifted up
to whirl in a vortex, seem to vaporize,
calling and falling in the blast. With our thud
to the ground we materialize
in a wet muddy treeless world
splintered with soaked, jagged boards.
All that we know is debris we *must*
climb out of—our wills still intact.
We're not new selves until we act.

IF YOU WANT TO LOOK ON THE BRIGHT SIDE

I don't have time for pointless
niceties.
I call a spade a spade.
Besides, I can always blame
my medication when it comes
right down to it.

But most people don't come
right down to it. Isn't that
the point?

You're an idiot.
I just say it plainly.
You are dumber than shit.
Yes, I mean you, asshole.
Now fuck off.

People praise you walking
in your own neighbourhood.
They praise you for eating
a full meal.
They praise you for brushing
your teeth, filling out a form,
& taking a shit.

People who never liked you,
people you never liked,
smile at you.
So happy are they that you've
reduced their odds.

Fuck you, asshole.
Yes, I mean you.

I can always blame
my medication when it comes
right down to it.

Besides, no one argues with me
anymore.

I can say whatever I want
& no one has the nerve to
contradict me.

I say it's snowing outside.
No need to look out the window.
Doesn't matter if it's 30 degrees plus.
It's snowing outside.

And every snowflake outside my window
is alike.

ANOTHER DYSFUNCTIONAL CANCER POEM

My body and I have now entered that phase
of relationship where all the quirks and tics
that used to tug at your heart are sources
of irritation and argument. The monotony of being
with you, day in and day out, going through the motions.
We are now that couple no one wants to
see in public, whose shopping bags hang like broken
promises. We blame each other's childhoods and
draft unacceptable separation agreements.
The hot tears and intermittent flowers are
the worst, the notes of distant affection,
the vague plans for future holidays. I am no
longer the love of your life. I have the black
eyes to prove it. Our pleas for forgiveness
are hollow. We live for the possibility of thrashing
it all out for the umpteenth time, falling asleep
exhausted and sore, but side by side.

BIOGRAPHICAL NOTES AND ACKNOWLEDGEMENTS

Nelson Ball's recent books are *Walking* (Mansfield Press, 2017), *Certain Details: The Poetry of Nelson Ball* selected with an introduction by Stuart Ross (Wilfrid Laurier University Press, 2017), and *A Vole on a Roll* with illustrations by JonArno Lawson (Shapes and Sounds Press, 2016). He lives in Paris, Ontario. "Chewing Water" and "Barbara Dying" appeared in *Chewing Water* (Mansfield Press, 2016).

Susie Berg has published two full-length poetry collections, *How to Get Over Yourself* and *All This Blood* (Piquant Press), and three chapbooks. She is the editor of the anthology *Catherines the Great*, forthcoming from Oolichan Books, and is writing her first novel. "Welcome Back to Cancerland" appeared in the collection *How to Get Over Yourself* (Piquant Press, 2013).

Samantha Bernstein is the author of a poetry collection, *Spit on the Devil* (Mansfield Press, 2017), and a memoir, *Here We Are Among the Living* (Tightrope Books, 2012), which was nominated for a BC National Award for Canadian Non-Fiction. She is at work on a book about the aesthetics of dereliction and compassion.

Becky Blake is a poetry ingenue and reluctant lymphoma aficionado who recently celebrated her five-year anniversary post-stem-cell transplant. Her debut novel is forthcoming from Wolsak & Wynn's Buckrider Books in spring 2019.

Ronna Bloom is a writer and psychotherapist whose sixth book of poetry is *The More* (Pedlar Press, 2017). Her poems have been recorded for CNIB and translated into Spanish and Bengali. She has collaborated with hospital workers, academics, filmmakers, and architects. Ronna is currently Poet in Residence in the Sinai Health System. "Open City" appeared in *The More*.

Christian Bök is the author of *Eunoia* (2001), a best-selling work of experimental literature that won the Griffin Prize for Poetic Excellence. Bök is a Fellow of the Royal Society of Canada, and he teaches at Charles Darwin University.

Sue Bracken's debut collection of poetry is *When Centipedes Dream* (Tightrope Books 2018), which included the first appearance of "Bounce." She says: "Although the content is serious, the power and joy of surviving is evidenced in the title. 'Bounce' was the perfect name for this poem, and for me."

Ronnie R. Brown is the author of six full-length poetry books and one chapbook. Her work has appeared in journals and anthologies in Canada, the U.S., and beyond. In 2006, Ronnie was awarded the People's Poetry Award for her collection *States of Matter* (Black Moss Press). Her breast cancer is now in remission.

Diana Fitzgerald Bryden is the author of a novel and two books of poetry, as well as numerous essays, poems, and short stories. She has recently completed her second novel, *Wet Dogs*, and is working on a set of short stories.

Susan Buis lives in the hills of the Thompson Nicola Valley in Interior British Columbia. Her writing has appeared in *Event, Prairie Fire, Vallum, Fiddlehead, CV2*, and *Malahat Review* and has won awards from some of these journals. A collection is forthcoming from Invisible Publishing in 2019.

Jane Byers has published two poetry collections, *Acquired Community*, (2016, Caitlin Press–Dagger Editions), a 2017 Goldie Award Winner for Poetry, and *Steeling Effects* (2014, Caitlin Press). Jane has had poems and essays published in literary journals in Canada, the U.S., and England, including *Best Canadian Poetry in English 2014*.

Natalee Caple is the author of eight books of poetry and fiction and the co-editor of an anthology of interviews with Canadian authors. Her newest book of poetry, *Love in the Chthulcene / Cthulhucene*, is forthcoming with Wolsak & Wynn in 2019. She is a professor at Brock University.

Louise Carson's poetry has been published here and there, including in *The Best Canadian Poetry in English 2013*. Her collection *A Clearing* appeared in 2015. She also writes mysteries—*Executor, The Cat Among Us, The Cat Vanishes*; and historical fiction—*In Which, Measured*, and *Third Circle*, set in 18th-century Scotland.

Ron Charach is the author of ten books of poetry, most recently *Prosopagnosia* (face blindness), published by Tightrope Books. In 2017 Tightrope published his novel *cabana the big*. "A Poem about the Pancreas" appeared in *The Big Life Painting*, the anthology *The Naked Physician*, and *Selected Portraits* (Wolsak & Wynn). "Breakaway" appeared in *Forgetting the Holocaust* (Frontenac House).

Valerie Charnish's work has appeared in *Arc Poetry Magazine, The Tishman Review*, and *Cottage Life*. She divides her time between Wolfe Lake, Ontario, and Toronto. She was diagnosed with breast cancer while her mother was dying of the disease. This painful experience was the catalyst for her to write poetry.

David Clink's latest poetry collection is *The Role of Lightning in Evolution* (Chizine Publications, 2016). His poem "A sea monster tells his story" won the Aurora Award for Best Poem/Song in 2013. "My Response to Your Mayday Call," written with Herb Kauderer, is nominated for the Pushcart Prize.

Joan Conway has a deep respect for relationships in her northern B.C. community, which strongly influences her work. Her poetry has appeared in several publications and anthologies, including *Unfurled* (Caitlin Press), as well as "Poem in Your Pocket 2018" (League of Canadian Poets).

Linda Crosfield's work appears in literary magazines including *Room, Minnesota Review, Antigonish Review, New Orphic Review*, and in chapbooks and anthologies. An earlier version of "The Summer I'm Ten My Aunt Wears a Bright Blue Shirt" appeared in the 2009 chapbook *Tears, the Same Music: Poems from Ocean Wilderness*.

Nancy Jo Cullen has published three poetry collections with Calgary's Frontenac House and a story collection with Biblioasis. Her novel *The Western Alienation Merit Badge* is forthcoming (Wolsak & Wynn, 2019). She's at work on a new collection of poems with the working title *Nothing Will Save Your Life*.

Dina Del Bucchia is the author of the short story collection *Don't Tell Me What to Do* (Arsenal Pulp Press, 2018) and the poetry collections *Coping with Emotions and Otters* (Talonbooks, 2013), *Blind Items* (Insomniac Press, 2014), and *Rom Com* (Talonbooks, 2015), written with Daniel Zomparelli.

Josie Di Sciascio-Andrews is the host and coordinator of the Oakville Literary Café Series. Her new collection, *Sunrise Over Lake Ontario*, was published this year. Josie's poetry has been shortlisted for the *Malahat Review*'s Open Season Award, *Descant*'s Winston Collins Prize, and won first place in Arborealis and Big Pond Rumours online poetry journal.

Christopher Doda is the author of three collections of poetry, most recently *Glutton for Punishment* (Mansfield Press, 2018). He is also the Series Editor for the annual *Best Canadian Essays*.

Anita Dolman's debut short fiction collection is *Lost Enough* (Morning Rain Publishing, 2017). She is a contributing editor for *Arc Poetry Magazine* and co-edited *Motherhood in Precarious Times*, an anthology of non-fiction, essays and poetry (Demeter Press, 2018). A version of "Mastectomy" appeared in *Ottawater*.

Rishma Dunlop was a vivacious, sensual Canadian poet, and a much-loved professor of creative writing at York University. Her cancer was diagnosed on Saturday, April 22, 2012, and she lived till Sunday, April 17, 2016. "Post-Op Delirium" and "Rock Me" were the final two poems she worked on.

Beth Everest found *silent sister: the mastectomy poems* (Frontenac House, 2016) indubitably cathartic to write, but it has since opened many opportunities. Mostly, though, Beth is thrilled to learn that her new piece, "re:construct," will be published in the same anthology as her youngest daughter's poems.

Brian L. Flack has published three novels, *In Seed Time, With a Sudden & Terrible Clarity,* and *When Madmen Lead the Blind,* and a book of poems, *36...Poems* (Point Petre Publishing, 2017). For forty years, he was a professor of English literature. He lives in Prince Edward County, Ontario. "The Respirologist" and "The Thoracic Surgeon" appeared in *36...Poems.*

Kate Marshall Flaherty has been shortlisted for *Descant*'s Best Canadian Poem, the Pablo Neruda Poetry Prize, Thomas Merton Poetry of the Sacred Prize, Robert Frost Poetry Award, and others. She's Writer in Residence at the Heliconian Club and Toronto Rep, League of Canadian Poets.

Katerina Vaughan Fretwell's "No Room for Gloom" appeared in her eighth poetry book, *Dancing on a Pin* (Inanna Publications, 2015), which was part of Battle of the Bards, and five poems from which placed as runners-up in the *subTerrain* Outsider Contest, and was long-listed for the Lowther Prize. "No Room for Gloom" also appeared in *Scintilla #16.*

Pam Galloway lives in Vancouver, where walks through her neighbourhood often inspire poems. Pam's books of poetry are *Parallel Lines* (Ekstasis Editions, 2006) and *Passing Stranger* (Innana Publications, 2014). Her poems have also been published widely in literary magazines and anthologies and twice on the website of the Canadian Parliamentary Poet Laureate.

Kim Goldberg is the author of seven books of poetry and non-fiction. Her *Red Zone* collection of poems on urban homelessness has been taught in university literature courses. *Undetectable* is her haibun journey through a lifetime of hepatitis C. Kim lives, wanders, and beats the odds in Nanaimo, B.C.

Lily Gontard lives in Whitehorse, Yukon. Her writing has appeared in *Geist, The Puritan, Up Here,* and more. Her non-fiction book *Beyond Mile Zero* (Lost Moose/

Harbour Publishing, 2017) is a collaboration with photographer Mark Kelly exploring the vanishing Alaska Highway lodge community.

Catherine Graham is the author of the novel *Quarry* and six acclaimed poetry collections including *The Celery Forest* (Wolsak & Wynn, Buckrider Books), a CBC Books 2017 Best Canadian Poetry Book. Winner of IFOA's Poetry NOW, she teaches at the University of Toronto SCS. "Sheet Music for Breathing in the Radiation Room" and "MRI" appeared in *The Celery Forest*.

Andreas Gripp lives in London, Ontario, with his wife, Carrie, and their two cats, Mabel and Mila. His latest book is *Selected Poems 4th edition* (Harmonia Press, 2018).

Teva Harrison is an artist, writer, and cartoonist. She is the author of the critically acclaimed hybrid graphic memoir *In-Between Days* (House of Anansi Press), winner of the Kobo Emerging Writer Prize for Non-Fiction and shortlisted for the Governor General's Literary Award for Non-Fiction and the Joe Shuster Award for Cartoonist/Auteur.

James Hawes lives and writes in Montreal. His work has appeared in *Grain, Stone the Crows!, Quills, Rogue Stimulus* (Mansfield Press), and the *Wes Ander-Zine*. His first chapbook is *Bus Metro Walk* (Monk Press, 2018).

Cornelia Hoogland's "Trailer Park Elegy" was a finalist for the League of Canadian Poets' 2018 Raymond Souster Award. "Woods Wolf Girl" was a finalist for the 2012 ReLit Award for Poetry. Two recent finalists for the CBC Literary Prizes were "Tourists Stroll a Victoria Waterway" (poetry) and "Sea Level" (non-fiction). An earlier version of "Gravelly Bay" was published by the Alfred Gustav Press, 2012.

Louisa Howerow's poetry is included in various anthologies, among them *I Found It at the Movies: An Anthology of Film Poems* (Guernica Editions), *Imaginarium 4: The Best Canadian Speculative Writing* (ChiZine Publications), and *River of Earth and Sky: Poems for the Twenty-First Century* (Blue Light Press).

Maddy Hughes studies geological engineering at the University of British Columbia. This is her first publication.

Barbara E. Hunt applies her poet's heart to many genres. She has literary journals, anthologies, and magazines across North America, the U.K., and Australia to her credit; current writings (*free*) on WATTPAD and enjoys kudos for her second release, a poetry/colouring book called *Devotions* (2017).

Crystal Hurdle teaches English and creative writing at Capilano University in North Vancouver. In October 2007, she was Guest Poet at the International Sylvia Plath Symposium at the University of Oxford. *Teacher's Pets*, a teen novel in verse, was published in 2014. "Letters to the Insurance Adjuster" appeared in *Body Breakdowns: Tales of Illness + Recovery* (Anvil Press, 2007).

Doyali Islam is a 2017 National Magazine Award finalist whose poems have been published in *Kenyon Review Online*, CBC Radio's *The Sunday Edition*, and *The Best Canadian Poetry in English 2018*. Doyali's second poetry book, *heft* (McClelland & Stewart), is forthcoming in 2019. "site" won the grand prize in *Arc Poetry Magazine*'s 2016 Poem of the Year Contest and "sites" appeared in *PRISM international*.

Melanie Janisse-Barlow is a poet and artist. Her first poetry collection, *Orioles in the Oranges* (Guernica, 2009), was listed for the Relit Award, and her essay poems, *Detroit*, were listed in *Best American Essays* in 2013. She has published in anthologies and journals in Canada and the U.S. Her second poetry collection is *Thicket* (Ansthruther/Palimpsest Press, 2018). Melanie lives in Windsor and Toronto.

Poet/playwright **Penn Kemp** has been lauded as a trailblazer since her first Coach House publication (1972) and a "one-woman literary industry" as London's inaugural Poet Laureate, Western's Writer-in-Residence, and the League of Canadian Poets' Spoken Word Artist, 2015. Her 2018 books of poetry are *Local Heroes* and *Fox Haunts*. "Nursing Her Home" appeared in *Tuck Magazine*.

Norma Kerby has poetry published in journals, e-zines, and anthologies, most recently, *Prairie Journal* (Pushcart Prize nomination), *Fresh Voices, Somewhere My Love Anthology* (Subterranean Blues Poetry), *Tree Anthology* (League of Canadian Poets, June, 2018), and the chapbook *Shores of Haida Gwaii* (Big Pond Rumours, 2018).

Paula Kienapple-Summers lives in Kitchener, Ontario. Her poetry has been recognized three times by the Dorothy Shoemaker Literary Awards, and published in *Spadina Literary Review* and *Existere*. A cancer survivor, Paula is also a volunteer, gardener, and educator.

Jónína Kirton is a Métis/Icelandic poet. She lives in the unceded territory of the Musqueam, Skwxwú7mesh, and Tsleil-Waututh. Jónína received the 2016 Vancouver's Mayor's Arts Award for an Emerging Artist in the Literary Arts category. Her second poetry collection, *An Honest Woman*, was a finalist in the 2018 Dorothy Livesay Poetry Prize.

Glenn Kletke is an Ottawa writer and prostate cancer survivor. He believes that words will not cure things: "They do more. They help us find our way."

Aaron Kreuter is the author of the poetry collection *Arguments for Lawn Chairs* (Guernica Editions, 2016) and the short story collection *You and Me, Belonging* (Tightrope Books, 2018). He lives in Toronto. "Dreams I Had the Week Before My Grandmother Passed Away" appeared in *Hart House Review*.

Marie Lauzier has had an up-close relationship with cancer for decades: in adolescence as a niece and a daughter, much later as a sister-in-law, and more recently as a friend and a cancer patient herself. Through it all, she is always moved by the frail beauty of life.

Joanna Lilley is the author of two poetry collections, *If There Were Roads* (Turnstone Press) and *The Fleece Era* (Brick Books); a short story collection, *The Birthday Books* (Radiant Press); and a novel, *Worry Stones* (Ronsdale Press). Joanna's poems are dedicated to her sister, artist Rebecca Lilley, who died of breast cancer.

Margo Little, founder of the Manitoulin Writers' Circle and charter member of the Sudbury Writers' Guild, is an internationally published journalist and photographer. Recent titles include *Portraits of Spirit Island* and *Pilgrims at Poplar Corners*. Her poetry has appeared in *Sulphur* and *Our Lakes Shall Set Us Free*.

Lois Lorimer is a poet, actor, and teacher. Her poetry collection, *Stripmall Subversive*, was published in 2012. Her poems have appeared in *Arc, Literary Review of Canada*, and various anthologies. Treated for cancer at Princess Margaret Cancer Centre, Lois is grateful for the strides made in research, education, and prevention. "Rescue Dog" appeared in *The Bright Well* (Leaf Press, 2011).

Rupert Loydell is Senior Lecturer in English with Creative Writing at Falmouth University, the editor of *Stride* magazine, and a contributing editor to *international times*. His poetry books include *Dear Mary* and *The Return of the Man Who Has Everything* (both published by Shearsman). "Flesh and Fluids" appeared in *Endlessly Divisible* (Driftwood, 2003) and *An Experiment in Navigation* (Shearsman, 2008).

Canisia Lubrin is a writer, editor, and critic. She is the author of *Voodoo Hypothesis* (Wolsak & Wynn, 2017), finalist for the Gerald Lampert, Pat Lowther, and Raymond Souster awards, and named a CBC Best Book of the Year. "Numbers Less Than Zero" appeared in *Vallum*.

Moira MacDougall's poems are from her second collection, *Vanishing Acts*, arising from a family story in which four family members die in the span of a year, the narrator then suffering the same piece of cellular chaos and her husband shortly thereafter. Moira is the Poetry Editor of *Literary Review of Canada*.

Teegan Mannion is a mother, writer, therapeutic clown, a sunbather, planter of seeds, and lover of green things. She finds joy and meaning in expression and connection, using therapeutic arts to contribute to the creation of safe and supportive spaces and strong community, especially including populations who are marginalized and stigmatized.

Blaine Marchand's poetry has appeared in Canada, the U.S., and Pakistan. Active in Ottawa for over forty years, he was president of the League of Canadian Poets from 1991 to 1993. *My Head, Filled with Pakistan*, a chapbook, was published in 2016. Blaine is working on a manuscript, *Where You Dwell*, and a series, *Finding My Voice*.

Dave Margoshes is a Saskatoon-area writer whose work has appeared widely in Canadian literary magazines and anthologies, including three times in *Best Canadian Poetry in English*. His *Dimensions of an Orchard* won the 2010 Saskatchewan Book Awards Poetry Prize. A new collection, *A Calendar of Reckoning*, was published this spring by Coteau Books.

rob mclennan lives in Ottawa, where he is home full-time with the two wee girls he shares with Christine McNair. His most recent titles include the poetry collections *A perimeter* (New Star Books, 2016), *How the alphabet was made* (Spuyten Duyvil, 2018), and *Household items* (Salmon Poetry, 2018).

Susan McMaster's poetry publications include books, anthologies, and scripts; recordings with Geode Music & Poetry and First Draft intermedia; and collaborations with artists, dancers, dramatists, and composers. She's the founding editor of Canada's first feminist magazine, *Branching Out*, and a past president of the League of Canadian Poets. "Chaise" appeared in *Until the Light Bends* (Black Moss Press, 2004).

Ottawa author **James K. Moran**'s fiction and poetry have appeared in Canadian, American, and British publications including *Bywords*, *Icarus*, and *Glitterwolf*. His articles have appeared via CBC Radio, *Daily Xtra*, and *Rue Morgue*. *Town & Train* (Lethe Press, 2014) is his debut horror novel.

Pamela Mordecai writes for children and adults. She is committed to exploring many Englishes in her poetry, fiction, and plays, in particular the range of the Jamaican Creole continuum. Her recent poetry collections are *Subversive Sonnets* and *De Book of Mary*. Her debut novel, *Red Jacket*, was shortlisted for the Rogers Writers' Trust fiction award (2015).

A. F. Moritz's most recent books are *The Sparrow: Selected Poems* (2018) and *Sequence: a Poem* (2015), both from House of Anansi. In 2015, Princeton University Press reissued his 1986 volume, *The Tradition*, in the Princeton Legacy Series.

Barbara Myers has published poems, essays, and reviews in a wide variety of periodicals and anthologies. Her book *Slide* (Signature Editions, 2010) was shortlisted for the Archibald Lampman Award for Poetry. She lives in Ottawa amidst a large family.

Chris Nash is a retired Sudbury psychologist and breast cancer survivor who has been writing professionally for almost fifty years. She has published short stories; academic articles; newspaper columns; a best-selling book, *The Learning Environment* (MacMillan); and a novel, *Temperance Lloyd: Hanged for Witchcraft in 1682*.

Jim Nason is the author of six poetry collections—most recently, *Rooster, Dog, Crow* (Frontenac House). *Touch Anywhere to Begin* was a finalist for the 2017 Re-Lit Award in poetry. His third novel, *Spirit of a Hundred Thousand Dead Animals*, was published by Signature Editions in 2017.

Abby Paige is a writer and performer based in New Brunswick. She and her older sister were both treated for breast cancer in 2009 and made full recoveries. "The Irises" appeared in *carte blanche*.

Molly Peacock is a widely anthologized poet and biographer who began *The Best Canadian Poetry* series. Her latest collection is *The Analyst* (Biblioasis), poems that tell the story of a decades-long patient-therapist relationship that reverses and continues to evolve after the analyst's stroke and reclamation of her life through painting. "Health Storm" appeared in *The Windsor Review*.

Miranda Pearson is the author of four collections of poetry: *Prime* (Beach Holme 2001), *The Aviary* (2007), *Harbour* (2010), and *The Fire Extinguisher* (2015), all published by Oolichan Books. *Harbour* and *The Fire Extinguisher* were both nominated for the Dorothy Livesay Prize. Miranda lives in Vancouver, where she teaches and edits poetry and works in community mental health.

Kirsten Pendreigh's poetry appears in *CV2, subTerrain, Prairie Fire, Juniper*, and *The Sustenance Anthology* (Anvil Press). She lives on Vancouver's North Shore and strives to be the kind of person her dog thinks she is.

Rusty Priske's work has appeared in his two books (*Rusty Priske: Trapeze Artist* and *This Is Day One*), multiple chapbooks, eight CDs, and three issues of *Oratarealis*. His work in the Canadian spoken word community was recognized with the Zaccheus Jackson Nyce Memorial Award in 2018. He was diagnosed with stage 3 colon cancer in 2016.

D. C. Reid is a past president of the League of Canadian Poets where, through donating and fundraising, he started a P. K. Page Trust Fund for mentoring that nears $40,000, as well as the D. C. Reid Poets' Bursary Fund, which stands at $11,000. "An ode an elegy a cancer" appeared in his eighth book of poems, *These Elegies* (2018).

Mary Rykov is a Toronto writer, editor, and PEN Canada advocate whose poetry and prose appear in numerous print and web venues. Her first poetry collection, *some conditions apply*, launches in 2019 with Inanna Publications.

Sonia Saikaley is the author of *The Lebanese Dishwasher*. Her first collection of poetry was *Turkish Delight, Montreal Winter* (Mawenzi House, 2012), and a second collection, *A Samurai's Pink House*, was published in 2017. Her novel *The Allspice Bath* is slated for publication in 2019 (Inanna Publications). "Soldier" appeared in *Turkish Delight, Montreal Winter*.

Rebecca Salazar is the author of *Guzzle* (Anstruther, 2016), and has published poetry and non-fiction in journals recently, including *Prism, Minola*, and *The Puritan*. A poetry editor for *The Fiddlehead* and *Plenitude* magazines, she is a PhD candidate and Vanier scholar at the University of New Brunswick.

Eleonore Schönmaier's most recent book is *Dust Blown Side of the Journey* (McGill-Queen's University Press). Her poetry has been set to music by Canadian, Dutch, Scottish, American, and Greek composers and has been performed in concert by the New European Ensemble. "Thanksgiving" appeared in *Wavelengths of Your Song* (McGill-Queen's University Press, 2013).

Emily Schultz is the co-founder of *Joyland Magazine* and the author of the novel *The Blondes*, which was published in Canada, the U.S., and France, and named a Best Book by NPR. Her poetry collection, *Songs for the Dancing Chicken*, was a Trillium Award finalist. She now lives in Brooklyn. "Greater Than and Less Than" appeared in *Room Magazine*.

David Seymour has written two books of poetry, *Inter Alia* (Brick Books, 2005) and *For Display Purposes Only* (Coach House Books, 2013). He is at work on his third book, *Lens Flare*. "Nil by None" appeared in *For Display Purposes Only*.

Laurie Siblock lives in Cobourg, Ontario, and works at a pioneer village. She has been writing all her life. Laurie rang the bell in 2014. "Facing the Diagnosis, Calmly" appeared in *The Northern Testicle Review*.

Bardia Sinaee was born in Tehran, Iran, and lives in Toronto. His poems have appeared in publications across Canada, including *Maisonneuve, The Walrus*, and *Best Canadian Poetry in English*. He is an MFA student at Guelph-Humber. "Return to St. Joseph's" appeared in *The Puritan;* "Transfusion" appeared in *The Walrus*.

Cora Siré is the author of a poetry collection, *Signs of Subversive Innocents*, and two novels, *The Other Oscar* and *Behold Things Beautiful*. Her poems, essays, and stories have appeared in magazines such as *Arc Poetry, Literary Review of Canada, The Puritan*, and *Montréal Serai*, and in several anthologies.

Adam Sol has published four collections of poetry, including *Complicity* (McClelland & Stewart, 2014), *Jeremiah, Ohio* (House of Anansi, 2008), and *Crowd of Sounds* (House of Anansi, 2003). He also manages a blog, *How a Poem Moves*, which will appear in book form in 2019 from ECW Press.

Carol Harvey Steski's poems have appeared in *Room, Freefall, Prairie Fire*, and *CV2*, and Winnipeg Transit's "Poetry in Motion" initiative. She's also spoken on CBC Radio-Manitoba about the therapeutic benefits of writing through disease as a young adult survivor of melanoma. She lives in Toronto with her husband and daughter. An earlier version of the "Clog: A Series" appeared in *Prairie Fire*.

JC Sulzenko's poems appear on *Arc*'s Poem of the Year shortlist, in *Vallum, Oratorealis*, and *Maple Tree Literary Supplement*, and at *The Light Ekphrastic* and Silver Birch Press. *South Shore Suite...Poems* came out in 2017 (Point Petre Publishing). She serves on Bywords.ca' s selection board and curates the Glebe Report's "Poetry Quarter."

Moez Surani's writing has been published internationally, including in *Harper's Magazine, Best American Experimental Writing 2016, Best Canadian Poetry in En-*

glish, and the *Globe and Mail*. Most recently, he is the author of the poetry book *Operations* and the custom scent installation, *Heresies*. "Theseus & Aegeus" appeared in *Floating Life* (Wolsak & Wynn, 2012).

Dane Swan is the author of four books: two poetry collections, one short story collection, and one novella. His second poetry collection, *A Mingus Lullaby*, was a finalist for the 2017 Trillium Book Prize for Poetry. Currently, Dane is editing an anthology celebrating diversity in Canadian literature for Guernica Editions.

Whitney Sweet's work has appeared in *A&U Magazine, Mentor Me: Instruction and Advice for Aspiring Writers*, and the forthcoming anthology *Far Villages: Welcome Essays for New and Beginner Poets* from Black Lawrence Press. She is creator of *T.R.O.U. Lit. Mag.* and winner of the Judith Eve Gewrutz Memorial Poetry Award.

Richard Teleky is the author of twelve books, including two volumes of poetry, four novels, and a short-story collection, and non-fiction studies—most recently *The Blue Hour* and *Ordinary Paradise: Essays on Art and Culture*. His poetry and essays have appeared in journals in Canada and the U.S. "For Zoli" appeared in *The Hermit's Kiss* (Fitzhenry & Whiteside, 2006).

The poet laureate of Grand Rapids, Michigan, from 2007 to 2010, **Rodney Toreson**, along with Russell Thorburn, is the co-author of the poetry book *The Jukebox Was the Jury of Their Love*, coming soon from Finishing Line Press.

Barbara Tran dedicates her poem to you. She is deeply grateful to the Ontario Arts Council for support that enables her writing of poetry.

Rhea Tregebov is the author of seven collections of poetry, most recently *All Souls'*, as well as the historical novel *The Knife Sharpener's Bell*. She is working on a new manuscript of poetry and completing a second novel. She is an Associate Professor Emerita of Creative Writing at UBC. "Sonnet: Nausea" appeared in the online journal *Juniper*.

Naomi Wakan has written over fifty books including the trilogy *The Way of Haiku, The Way of Tanka*, and *Poetry That Heals*. She is the inaugural Poet Laureate of Nanaimo and the Inaugural Honorary Ambassador for the B.C. Federation of Writers. She lives on Gabriola Island. "Cancer Episode" appeared in *Bent Arm for a Pillow* (Pacific-Rim Publishers).

Anne F. Walker writes poems that concentrate attention on precision of image, narrative, and language. They reflect on landscapes and bodies and the memories rooted there. Her books include *Into the Peculiar Dark, Pregnant Poems, The Exit Show,* and the recent chapbook *when the light of any action ceases.* "Swallow" appeared in *Into the Peculiar Dark* (The Mercury Press and bpNichol Foundation).

Myna Wallin is the author of *A Thousand Profane Pieces* (Tightrope Books, 2006), *Confessions of a Reluctant Cougar* (Tightrope Books, 2010), and *Anatomy of an Injury* (Inanna Publications, 2018). "Dinner Theatre" appeared in *Anatomy of an Injury.*

Zoe Whittall is the author of three novels, most recently the Giller-nominated *The Best Kind of People,* which will soon be a feature film by Sarah Polley. Her latest book of poetry was *Precordial Thump.* Her forthcoming novel is called *The Spectacular.*

Jocelyn Williams is a writer, parent, and professor. Her opponent is breast cancer but her victory is in truth-telling and fresh air. She rises to see her daughters create and her teaching encourages kinship. Jocelyn has published research and creative work in Canadian and international journals, including *TAR* and *Canadian Woman Studies.*

Elana Wolff is a Toronto-based writer of poetry and creative non-fiction, editor, and designer and facilitator of social art courses. Her work has appeared in Canadian and international publications and has garnered awards. Her most recent poetry collection is *Everything Reminds You of Something Else* (Guernica Editions, 2017).

Anna Yin was Mississauga's first poet laureate (2015–16). She has four poetry collections and won two MARTY Awards, WCU Poetry Conference scholarships, and Ontario Art Council grants. Her poems have appeared in *Arc Poetry, New York Times, China Daily, CBC Radio, World Journal, Literary Review of Canada.* "Snow" appeared in *Seven Nights with the Chinese Zodiac* (Black Moss Press, 2015).

Kurt Zubatiuk is a poet, psychotherapist, Mediaeval fencer, and author of *Ekstasis* (LyricalMyrical 2007). Kurt is a graduate of the Toronto Institute for Relational Psychotherapy and is a registered psychotherapist in Toronto. "Took You in Pieces" appeared in a different form in the anthology *Renaissance Conspiracy* (Micro Prose, 2004).

ACKNOWLEDGEMENTS

We are grateful to all of the writers who contributed to this groundbreaking book: we are filled with gratitude for your talents and your generosity of spirit.

A big, heartfelt thanks to Denis De Klerck and Mansfield Press for publishing this anthology. And special thanks to Stuart Ross for his careful copy-editing and support. Thank you to Dr. Mary Jane Esplen, director of the de Souza Institute, for her belief in the importance of this book. Kristin Valois, thank you for your time and positivity.

Priscila and Meaghan would also like to thank their friends and family for the light and love they continue to give to us each and every day.

Photo: Daniel Ehrenworth

Meaghan Strimas is the author of three poetry collections, *Junkman's Daughter, A Good Time Had by All*, and *Yes or Nope*, which was awarded the Trillium Book Award for Poetry in 2017. Strimas is also the editor of *The Selected Gwendolyn MacEwen*. She is a professor and coordinator of English and Professional Writing & Communications at Humber College's Lakeshore campus, and the editor of the *Humber Literary Review*. Strimas is at work on a novel (*The Other Half*) and her fourth book of poems (*Make It Stop*). She lives in Toronto with her family.

Priscila Uppal was a Toronto poet, fiction writer, memoirist, essayist, playwright, Professor of English at York University, and a Fellow of the Royal Society of Canada. *Time Out London* dubbed her "Canada's coolest poet." Among her critically acclaimed publications are ten collections of poetry, most recently *Sabotage, Traumatology*, and *Ontological Necessities* (Griffin Poetry Prize finalist); the novels *The Divine Economy of Salvation* and *To Whom It May Concern*; the study *We Are What We Mourn: The Contemporary English-Canadian Elegy*; the memoir *Projection: Encounters with My Runaway Mother* (Writers' Trust Hilary Weston Prize and Governor General's Award finalist); the collection of short stories *Cover Before Striking*, and the play *6 Essential Questions*. Her work has been published internationally and translated into Croatian, Dutch, French, Greek, Hungarian, Italian, Korean, and Latvian. She was the first-ever poet-in-residence for Canadian Athletes Now during the 2010 Vancouver and 2012 London Olympic and Paralympic games as well as the Roger's Cup Tennis Tournament in 2011. Her second play, *What Linda Said*, had its world premiere at SummerWorks 2017. She was also editor of several anthologies including *Writing Creative Writing: Essays from the Field* (co-edited with Rishma Dunlop and Daniel Scott Tysdal). "If You Want to Look on the Bright Side" and "Another Dysfunctional Cancer Poem" appeared in *What Linda Said: Poems* (Gap Riot, 2017) and *On Second Thought* (Mansfield Press, 2018). Priscila died in September 2018 of synovial sarcoma, a rare form of cancer.